ADHD

ADHD

Paul Graves Hammerness

Biographies of Disease
Julie K. Silver, M.D., Series Editor

GREENWOOD PRESS
Westport, Connecticut • London

Library of Congress Cataloging-in-Publication Data

Hammerness, Paul Graves.
  ADHD / Paul Graves Hammerness.
    p. cm. — (Biographies of disease, ISSN 1940–445X)
  Includes bibliographical references and index.
  ISBN 978–0–313–34302–5 (alk. paper)
  1. Attention-deficit hyperactivity disorder. I. Title.
RJ506.H9H34485   2009
618.92′8589—dc22   2008032987

British Library Cataloguing in Publication Data is available.

Library of Congress Catalog Card Number: 2008032987
ISBN: 978-0-313-34302-5
ISSN: 1940–445X

First published in 2009

Greenwood Press, 88 Post Road West, Westport, CT 06881
An imprint of Greenwood Publishing Group, Inc.
www.greenwood.com

Printed in the United States of America

The paper used in this book complies with the
Permanent Paper Standard issued by the National
Information Standards Organization (Z39.48–1984).

10 9 8 7 6 5 4 3 2 1

This book would not be possible without the love and support of my family.

Contents

Series Foreword

Every disease has a story to tell: about how it started long ago and began to disable or even take the lives of its innocent victims, about the way it hurts us, and about how we are trying to stop it. In this Biographies of Disease series, the authors tell the stories of the diseases that we have come to know and dread.

The stories of these diseases have all of the components that make for great literature. There is incredible drama played out in real-life scenes from the past, present, and future. You'll read about how men and women of science stumbled trying to save the lives of those they aimed to protect. Turn the pages and you'll also learn about the amazing success of those who fought for health and won, often saving thousands of lives in the process.

If you don't want to be a health professional or research scientist now, when you finish this book you may think differently. The men and women in this book are heroes who often risked their own lives to save or improve ours. This is the biography of a disease, but it is also the story of real people who made incredible sacrifices to stop it in its tracks.

Julie K. Silver, M.D.
Assistant Professor, Harvard Medical School
Department of Physical Medicine and Rehabilitation

Preface

The purpose of this book is to introduce readers to the topic of attention deficit hyperactivity disorder (ADHD). This book spans the life course of the study of ADHD, from the initial serendipitous finding of stimulant response to the latest scientific advances and the subsequent directions of the field. Information collected for this book comes from the scientific literature, including professional guidelines, expert review, peer-reviewed journals, and clinical communications. The author reviews and summarizes this literature, given his research and clinical experience, including extensive work with children, adolescents, and adults with ADHD. The book follows the development of the field, with an initial description of the history of ADHD and its treatments followed by chapters outlining the core nature of the disorder and associated problems. A chapter on treatment follows a review of the drug development process so that readers have a sense of how treatments become available for a given condition. The book ends with discussion of recent advances in the field, including genetic investigations, brain imaging, and the understanding of how ADHD may continue into adulthood.

1

What Is Attention Deficit Hyperactivity Disorder (ADHD)?

INTRODUCTION

Are you paying attention? Ignore that person walking by you. Keep reading, but don't forget that you have a report to write after reading this. And, when you write the report, please spell the author's name carefully. If you must take a break (try to stick with this, it has only been a couple minutes so far!) do not misplace this book. Are you listening? Make sure you remember what time it is, and the other things you need to do today. OK, let's review, what were your instructions? The instructions were, again, to 1) pay attention; 2) don't get distracted; 3) don't forget about your report; 4) pay attention to details; 5) do not lose this book; 6) listen; and 7) be organized. Wait a minute, where are you going, sit back down!

When you stop and think about it, the human brain is remarkable in its "simple" ability to pay attention. But many of us do not pay attention to our ability to pay attention. It is taken for granted. But this ability defines us in a very profound way. Pay attention to reading this book, pay attention when crossing the street, pay attention to your lottery ticket, pay attention to what you are saying, did you say "I love you?," pay attention to details, when is the final for this class? Paying attention is important. But for some children, and adults, this does not come easily. And that can cause problems. Does that make intuitive sense? This is the fundamental nature of attention deficit hyperactivity disorder (ADHD).

ADHD is a collection of specific symptoms (e.g., inattention, distractibility, impulsivity, hyperactivity) beginning early in a person's life that are unusual as compared with peers and that typically occur wherever the individual is (e.g., home, school) and cause significant problems. Historically, ADHD has been considered to be a disorder of childhood. However, it has become quite clear that many children do not "grow out of it," and ADHD can continue to cause tremendous problems for an individual well into adulthood.

For the purposes of this book, and acknowledging that the bulk of the literature on ADHD deals with children, I will primarily refer to young persons with ADHD as a "child" with ADHD. This reference to "child" will encompass all pediatric age groups, through adolescence, unless there are special topics that would apply only to adolescents (such as driving) or adults. In addition, I will refer to ADHD as a "psychiatric disorder," which is consistent with the American Psychiatric Association's language for categorizing emotional, behavioral, and cognitive problems. I will use the pronoun "we" to refer to the community of doctors and researchers of which I am part. However, the information gathered here is based upon my personal, current understanding of ADHD, upon the literature, and upon my clinical experience working with children, adults, and families and is not intended to represent the views of all others involved in this field.

Finally, given my training as a physician, and my clinical work as a child and adolescent psychiatrist, the approach to and discussion of ADHD is primarily from a medical viewpoint. Although the emphasis is on the serious problems that can occur with ADHD, this is not to suggest that the diagnosis of ADHD for all children and adults will universally yield bad outcomes. I wish to emphasize that the public and scientific community should prioritize the assessment and treatment of psychiatric disorders in childhood.

Finally, from time to time in this text, I will consider issues surrounding ADHD as *scientific challenges* we can all work toward solving. In so doing, you can join the scientific study of ADHD, apply your ideas to this fascinating area of medicine, or apply some of these principles to other areas of interest. Reports can be generated using some of these topics as starting points. Your independent research can lead to advances in ADHD and perhaps to a career in child and adolescent psychiatry.

THE BIG VIEW

The big view is that ADHD can affect any child or any adult, in any place in the world. It is important to understand that ADHD is a condition that occurs worldwide. ADHD is not just seen in the United States (U.S.). The naming of the "disorder" may vary, it may not be called ADHD in every country, but the children's problems are quite similar wherever they are encountered. Most disorders can be thought of as having both genetic (what is inherited from a child's parents/families) and environmental (social and cultural demands, expectations, stressors, exposures) influences. The combination of genetic and environmental factors in a given area or country may be different and may affect how people describe, understand, and name the disorder, ADHD. However, contrary with what may be claimed by certain media or groups in this country (that ADHD is a made-up problem in the U.S.), well-informed medical professionals throughout the world agree that ADHD is a true neurobiological disorder.

ADHD symptoms can occur in any place. Over the past decades, ADHD has been one of the most studied childhood conditions in the U.S., with a growing understanding that symptoms of ADHD, such as inattention and impulsivity, can impact a child's functioning in any setting. In the past, ADHD was thought of as a school-based problem only. The idea was that the only place where being "spacey" or "hyper" mattered was in the classroom. Or better said, it was very important for children to be still, and listen to their elders, in the classroom. Currently, ADHD is appreciated as a condition with broad impact, across all areas of a child's life. As was mentioned at the beginning of this chapter, paying attention is important in every aspect of life.

For example, a child who is not paying attention in baseball may be asked to leave the team, a girl who is too hyperactive in girl scouts may be picked on by her peers, a boy who is not listening to directions around the home may be yelled at by his parents, a teenage girl who is distracted very easily may get into a car accident when driving. Impulsivity may lead to taking illegal drugs without thinking about the dangers. All these problems in all these different areas of a child's life may add up and cause much sadness, worry, or frustration.

ADHD can happen at any time in one's life. We understand now that ADHD symptoms can persist throughout a person's lifetime, as can other chronic medical or psychiatric conditions, like asthma or depression. The symptoms of ADHD may appear differently over the course of one's life, but the effect on an individual's life may be just as serious in adulthood as in childhood. Impulsivity may be noticeable by others in childhood, causing great problems in classrooms and contributing to high rates of injuries and accidents. ADHD's impairment in adulthood may be more to the result of inattention and disorganization, causing problems with relationships, work performance, and finances. ADHD is now thought of as a chronic condition, and the study of ADHD spans the entire life.

OUR GOALS

In this book, we will begin looking at the fascinating infancy of ADHD, tracing the birth of the disorder back to the 1800s. We will continue on to see how the study of ADHD matured, becoming one of the most studied childhood conditions. The story will end with the adulthood of ADHD, fully maturing into a disorder that is considered a worldwide condition, is present throughout life, and occurs at any place or time in an individual's life. We will end by looking into the future of ADHD, as we try to understand the causes of ADHD and how the disorder can be best treated. All treatment efforts are designed to move the ADHD child or adult into equilibrium with his/her most healthy, positive, and productive environment.

HISTORICAL OVERVIEW

"Let me see if Philip can be a little gentleman;
Let me see if he is able to sit still for once at table."

Der Struwwelpeter (1845)

ADHD has had many names over its lengthy history, including hyperkinesis, minimal brain damage or dysfunction, and attention deficit disorder (ADD) with or without hyperactivity. Over time, the lack of obvious, observable brain damage in children with ADHD led the field from its roots in thinking of it neurologically ("minimal brain damage") to follow the influence of psychiatry, psychology, and education ("ADHD").

The current scientific name is ADHD in this country, according to the American Psychiatric Association, which includes three "subtypes": = ADHD inattentive type, ADHD hyperactive-impulsive type, or ADHD combined type, with each referring to a collection of symptoms. The main symptoms of ADHD are primarily defined on the basis of behavior that can be observed by others. Although there are a total of eighteen ADHD symptoms, symptoms are organized into two main types, inattention (e.g., inattentive, distracted, disorganized) and hyperactivity-impulsivity (e.g., fidgety, talkative, hyperactive). Throughout the remainder of this historical review, the term ADHD will be used to represent the underlying commonality of these differently named disorders over time.

When thinking about the complex nature of the human brain and the basic differences between people, such as in intelligence, physical abilities, and artistic creativity, it makes intuitive sense that there would also be differences in individuals' abilities to pay attention, to think and act, at the most basic level. It makes sense that there have always been people who cannot pay attention to a task as long as others or who could not sit still as well as others. Consistent with this, one can trace ADHD back to early nineteenth-century observations of children and how they differed in behavior.

Poems from the early 1800s demonstrate that these behavioral differences among children were observed far before there was a common scientific name for the problem. For example, *Der Struwwelpeter* (1845), a popular German children's book by the physician Heinrich Hoffmann, included an illustrated story about "Fidgety Philip" (*Zappelphillip*) and "John-Head-in-Air" (*Hans-Guck-in-die-Luft*). Children with ADHD over time were referred to as having the "Zappelphillip-Syndrom." As an interesting side note, these stories by Dr. Hoffmann have been translated into several languages, including an English version by Mark Twain:

The Story of Fidgety Philip

"Let me see if Philip can
Be a little gentleman;
Let me see if he is able
To sit still for once at table":
Thus Papa bade Phil behave;
And Mamma looked very grave.
But fidgety Phil,
He won't sit still;
He wriggles,
And giggles,
And then, I declare,
Swings backwards and forwards,
And tilts up his chair,
Just like any rocking horse—
"Philip! I am getting cross!"

See the naughty, restless child
Growing still more rude and wild,
Till his chair falls over quite.
Philip screams with all his might,
Catches at the cloth, but then
That makes matters worse again.
Down upon the ground they fall,
Glasses, plates, knives, forks, and all.
How Mamma did fret and frown,
When she saw them tumbling down!

And Papa made such a face!
Philip is in sad disgrace.

Where is Philip, where is he?
Fairly covered up you see!
Cloth and all are lying on him;
He has pulled down all upon him.
What a terrible to-do!
Dishes, glasses, snapt in two!
Here a knife, and there a fork!
Philip, this is cruel work.
Table all so bare, and ah!
Poor Papa, and poor Mamma
Look quite cross, and wonder how
They shall have their dinner now.

Symptoms of hyperactivity-impulsivity can be found in Phil's behavior, just as we see in children who are diagnosed with ADHD these days. Phil is unable to sit still even for one meal at the table, constantly fidgety, moving about in his chair to the point of falling off it. Parents of children with ADHD to this day will often describe their child's level of activity as nonstop for the majority of the day, even when the child is supposed to be doing something as simple as sitting in a chair. Even for brief meals, it is not unusual for parents to describe the child with ADHD to be literally standing, not sitting, or using the chair as some form of play tool, like a gymnastic apparatus.

The Story of Johnny Head-In-Air

As he trudged along to school,
It was always Johnny's rule
To be looking at the sky
And the clouds that floated by;
But what just before him lay,
In his way,
Johnny never thought about;
So that every one cried out
"Look at little Johnny there,
Little Johnny Head-In-Air!"

Running just in Johnny's way
Came a little dog one day;

Johnny's eyes were still astray
Up on high,
In the sky;
And he never heard them cry
"Johnny, mind, the dog is nigh!"
Bump!
Dump!
Down they fell, with such a thump,
Dog and Johnny in a lump!

Once, with head as high as ever,
Johnny walked beside the river.
Johnny watched the swallows trying
Which was cleverest at flying.
Oh! what fun!
Johnny watched the bright round sun
Going in and coming out;
This was all he thought about.
So he strode on, only think!
To the river's very brink,
Where the bank was high and steep,
And the water very deep;
And the fishes, in a row,
Stared to see him coming so.

One step more! oh! sad to tell!
Headlong in poor Johnny fell.
And the fishes, in dismay,
Wagged their tails and swam away.

Oh! you should have seen him shiver
When they pulled him from the river.
He was in a sorry plight!
Dripping wet, and such a fright!
Wet all over, everywhere,
Clothes, and arms, and face, and hair:
Johnny never will forget
What it is to be so wet.

And the fishes, one, two, three,
Are come back again, you see;
Up they came the moment after,

> To enjoy the fun and laughter.
> Each popped out his little head,
> And, to tease poor Johnny, said
> "Silly little Johnny, look,
> You have lost your writing-book!"

In this brief poem, symptoms of inattention consistent with ADHD can be found in Johnny's behavior. Johnny does not pay attention to what is before him, and instead his eyes are astray, distracted by a cloud in the sky. Parents of children with ADHD to this day will often describe the child as rarely paying attention to the task at hand, whether it is homework, playing soccer, or walking the dog. Instead, parents describe the child as being distracted by anything, whether a cloud, a sound, or a piece of lint on the floor: "It is like he cannot ignore it at all."

Early Twentieth Century: Dr. Still's Abnormal Defect of Moral Control

Upon entering the twentieth century, the abnormal behaviors of children like Phil and Johnny were assumed to be caused by a brain injury. This was partly because of the observance of abnormal behavior in children with known brain damage. However, hyperactivity-impulsivity symptoms were found in children who had no known brain damage. In these children, the damage to the brain was still assumed to be present, just not detectable. The term "minimal brain damage" emerged as a scientific diagnosis for these children who were so different from "normal" or "healthy" children.

A more official, public beginning of ADHD study can be traced back to this period of time, specifically the year 1902. It was at this time that the British pediatrician Dr. George F. Still gave a lecture at a scientific meeting, the Royal College of Physicians of London, entitled "Some abnormal psychical conditions in children." Dr. Still is a perfect name for a doctor working with children with ADHD, trying to help the child sit *still*.

In his lectures, Dr. Still described "an abnormal defect of moral control in children," calling "urgently for scientific investigation." Dr. Still discussed abnormal behaviors in children who were known to be otherwise healthy, with normal intelligence. Dr. Still defined moral control as "the control of action in conformity with this moral consciousness ... a consciousness of the relation of every volitional activity on the part of the individual to the good of all." These (ADHD) children were not in conformity with general moral consciousness.

Dr. Still used descriptive cases of children to illustrate his points. Interestingly, the descriptions included reference to how these children were not functioning well in the community and in school. Dr. Still said that "a common history is that the child has been tried at various schools and at each fresh school has seemed for a time to have overcome his morbid propensities but not sooner have the surroundings become *commonplace and familiar* than some fresh manifestation ... leads to his disgrace and early expulsion."

This observance by Dr. Still raises an important point that we can discuss for a moment. The term attention deficit seems to imply that children with ADHD cannot pay attention at all. This is of course not the case. Children with ADHD can pay attention. However, they cannot consistently pay attention, over time, and in a variety of settings, like other children. Therefore, as described by Dr. Still, these children can focus in a new classroom, as they find new friends and new games. But then quite quickly they can lose that focus. The inattention, talkativeness, impulsivity, and restlessness can come roaring back, even though it seemed to be briefly gone. At present day, it is not unusual for children with ADHD to respond well to a new situation like a new classroom, which can hold their interest because of its novelty for a limited period of time.

In addition, Dr. Still noted that these children need "constant and close supervision" (Still, 1902). To this day, parents with very hyperactive children are often quite concerned about basic safety and either provide constant supervision or limit the child's activities. For example, parents may stop bringing their child to a local shopping mall after the child's repetitive impulsive dashes across the parking lot without looking for cars or impulsively adventuring off without the parent's company and becoming lost.

Mid-Twentieth Century: Dr. Charles Bradley's Arithmetic Pills

A short time after Dr. Still's influential teachings, in the 1930s, the first treatment for ADHD was stumbled upon. George Lathrop Bradley (1883–1906), a friend of Alexander Graham Bell, was a wealthy officer of the early telephone industry (AT&T). Mr. Bradley's only child, Emma, became seriously ill with an inflammation of the brain (encephalitis). After the illness, Emma had severe behavior problems and seizures. The generous financial gifts by her parents supported scientific study of serious childhood behavioral problems. Emma's parents eventually even supported the building of a children's home in Providence, Rhode Island, where George, Emma's father, came from.

The Emma P. Bradley Home (now Hospital) was opened in the early 1930s. The second head doctor of the home was a pediatrician, Charles Bradley, M.D., a cousin of George Bradley, the original founder of the home. Charles Bradley studied neurology, the brain, and the nervous system in his medical training. After his training, Charles studied the children whose behavioral problems led to their admission to the Emma Bradley Home (Work, 2001). Children could be admitted for a long hospitalization as doctors tried to understand how to treat these children in hopes that they might lead more healthy lives.

In the 1930s, x-rays of the head (pneumoencephalograms) were used to study the brains of children at the Emma P. Bradley Home. These x-rays involved injecting air through a needle into the back (spinal column) of a child. When the child sat up to allow air to rise up through the spinal column toward the brain, the x-ray could be taken. This procedure could be painful and caused headaches. During the hunt for treatments for the children's headaches, the doctors tried a common treatment for allergies and asthma, a medication called benzedrine. To the doctor's surprise, the medication helped the children study. In fact, the children called the medication "arithmetic pills." Benzedrine is a "stimulant," the same type of medication currently most effective in the treatment of ADHD.

Leaping ahead to the present day for a moment, scientific studies of new medications for ADHD include assessments of children's math abilities as a direct way of observing how much a child's attention is improved after taking an ADHD medication. Researchers measure how many math problems are attempted and how many are correctly done. The number of math problems attempted (and done correctly) by the child before receiving an ADHD medication is compared with the number of math problems attempted (and done correctly) after the child receives the medication. Results can be quite impressive, even after just one dose of medication. We will consider why this is the case in a later chapter.

Now back to Dr. Bradley. So dramatic were the observations of Bradley and his colleagues that the use of this medication was reported in the influential scientific journal, *The American Journal of Psychiatry*, in 1937 in the paper "The Behavior of Children Receiving Benzedrine." The paper reportedly did not provoke much attention at the time, despite the fact that it described the "paradox" that a stimulant was somehow capable of calming hyperactive children.

Ritalin, Mind Control, and the Loss of Causality

Stimulant medications are the class of medication that were discovered to be so effective in calming and focusing children with ADHD symptoms. There are two main types of stimulants, methylphenidates and amphetamines. One of the most well-known of this type of medications, Ritalin (a methylphenidate), was introduced into the public mainstream market in 1955. Although the scientific-medical community was making progress in understanding ADHD, at the time, there was increasing public concern about "mind control" and "drugging" children for the sake of a quiet, well-mannered classroom.

The same concerns of "drugging our children with powerful medications" can be heard today in the media and public conversation about ADHD. Contrary with some common perceptions, however, at the time when Ritalin emerged as a common treatment, child psychiatrists were openly concerned about the climate of drug abuse and the possibility that Ritalin might increase illegal drug use. Contrary with the fears that these prescription medications would become drugs of abuse, research has shown that stimulant treatment of ADHD can have no impact or actually reduce drug abuse. Nevertheless, psychiatrists are quite aware of the serious nature of diagnosis and treatment of children and weigh the risks and benefits of treating children with medications thoughtfully.

By the 1960s, efforts to best characterize ADHD led to the term "minimal brain *dysfunction*." By calling ADHD a "brain dysfunction" one could avoid the suggestion that there was a specific, known brain damage to account for the behavioral symptoms. However, this name too was soon discarded. By the late 1960s, the American Psychiatric Association coined the term "hyperkinetic reaction of childhood." This new name did not make any reference to brain injury, and as such the field moved away from any suggestion of known causality (identifiable brain damage) of the disorder. Further, the symptoms included in the disorder's diagnostic criteria were more limited, centering on behavioral manifestations such as overactivity, restlessness, and distractibility instead of broadly including other areas such as learning disabilities.

In the early 1970s, there were efforts to join the different historical roots of ADHD, acknowledging the historical role of the study of learning disorders as well as brain damage research. In one representative interdisciplinary (different fields of study) conference of that time period, experts gathered to establish criteria for diagnosis and consider directions of study. The series of papers later published from that conference is fascinating, in that scientists coming together to discuss ADHD presented such varied information. Scientists conjectured that ADHD may be caused by abnormal brain processing, akin to software programming dysfunction. The brain wiring, so to speak, could be damaged, even if the brain itself appeared normal in shape and size. This is quite consistent with some of the latest ideas on the cause of ADHD.

Scientists also emphasized that, because behavioral abnormalities such as ADHD could be found in multiple members of the same family, genetic factors were likely contributing to the presence of ADHD. At that time, researchers were also reporting on the use of stimulant medications in animal research, observing dogs to be behaviorally calmer after administration of the stimulant amphetamine. Others raised the concern that the ADHD child's immature or abnormal brain development could results in a child's total disequilibrium with the environment. This is contrary with the idea that impulsivity is an intentional behavior of a willful, stubborn, or deviant child. Much progress was being made.

Consistent with scientific efforts at understanding these children better, attempts were made to provide educational assistance by classifying ADHD as a form of learning disorder. Despite good intelligence, these children still greatly struggled in the classroom setting, not meeting behavioral and academic expectations. Again, reflecting the richness of study in the field, during this time period, clinicians developed opportunities for children with ADHD to develop mastery and skills through personalized educational programming. Emphasis was upon providing a routine, standard environment to help with organization and attention and minimize the bits of information being presented to the child at one time. You can imagine the beneficial impact of a smaller classroom, with excellent routines and expectations and with simple and direct directions versus the large, chaotic, ever-changing world of some school systems.

Back to the steady march of new names and new diagnostic classifications. In the early 1980s, a new name had emerged, ADD. Depending on the symptoms, the child was classified as having ADD with hyperactivity or ADD without hyperactivity. A focus on attention became evident; hyperactivity was no longer the primary symptom of concern. This name is recent enough that it is still often referred to with some degree of confusion. For example, "my child has ADD" can be stated by parents when trying to differentiate their child from one who is "hyper." Generally speaking, although there are differences at the symptom level in children with and without hyperactivity, fundamentally, children with ADHD (with or without the H) respond similarly to treatment and are considered to have more similarities than differences.

Despite the progression of study and understanding of ADHD, by the 1990s, a societal "war" broke out over the usage of the ADHD stimulant Ritalin. Articles and books condemned the use of these pills. The medications were thought to be uniformly inappropriately given to boys "who were just being boys." Ritalin was considered by some as a medication that did not treat a true genetic disorder of brain functioning but instead *caused* brain damage and created illegal drug abuse. The weight of the scientific evidence to date has not supported these suggestions or fears.

Attention Deficit Hyperactivity Disorder (ADHD)

The latest and most current terminology for the disorder came at the end of the twentieth century. The name remained descriptive, without implication of known cause, such as brain damage. According to the American Psychiatric Association's *Diagnostic and Statistical Manual*, a child who shows six or more symptoms of inattention (as below) for a duration of six months with onset before age seven meets the criteria for ADHD, inattentive type. A child who shows six or more symptoms of hyperactivity-impulsivity (as below) for a duration of six months with onset before age seven meets the criteria for ADHD, hyperactive-impulsive type. A child who shows six or more symptoms of inattention and six or more symptoms of hyperactivity-impulsivity (as below) for a duration of six months with onset before age seven meets the criteria for ADHD, combined type. Symptoms must be present in a persistent pattern for at least six months and must occur to a degree that is more frequent and more severe than in other children (individuals) at a comparable level of development.

Inattention symptoms:

1. often fails to give close attention to details or makes careless mistakes in schoolwork, work, or other activities
2. often has difficulty sustaining attention in tasks or play activities
3. often does not seem to listen when spoken to directly
4. often does not follow through on instructions and fails to finish schoolwork, chores, or duties in the workplace (not due to oppositional behavior or failure to understand instructions)
5. often has difficulty organizing tasks and activities
6. often avoids, dislikes, or is reluctant to engage in tasks that require sustained mental effort (such as schoolwork or homework)
7. often loses things necessary for tasks or activities (e.g., toys, school assignments, pencils, books, or tools)
8. is often easily distracted by extraneous stimuli
9. is often forgetful in daily activities

Hyperactive symptoms:

1. often fidgets with hands or feet or squirms in seat
2. often leaves seat in classroom or in other situations in which remaining seated is expected
3. oftens runs about or climbs excessively in situations in which it is inappropriate (in adolescents or adults, may be limited to subjective feelings of restlessness)
4. often has difficulty playing or engaging in leisure activities quietly
5. is often "on the go" or often acts as if "driven by a motor"
6. often talks excessively

Impulsive symptoms

1. often blurts out answers before questions have been completed
2. often has difficulty awaiting turn
3. often interrupts or intrudes on others (e.g., butts into conversations or games)

Twenty-First Century: Into the Future

[ADHD is a] neurobiological disorder. . . .
[whose] existence no longer should be debated.

World Federation for Mental Health

In this book, ADHD will be presented as a medical, genetically based disorder, as standing on a firm body of scientific evidence, with an ongoing dedication to research on the condition into the twenty-first century. As will be discussed in a later chapter, scientific study of ADHD in the twenty-first century includes a concerted effort to determine the specific genetic causes of ADHD, to identify the brain dysfunction at a cellular and biochemical level, to best track the impact of ADHD upon a child's functioning, and to optimally treat the disorder with a comprehensive plan, including advances in delivery systems for medication.

ADHD is now understood to be a chronic condition, much like asthma or diabetes, and as such, treatment must be broad, involving individual families, communities, and health care systems. Contrary with the 1800s, in which children with ADHD-like symptoms were likely expelled from schools and society or suffered serious injury, present-day children with ADHD can function in the presence of their peers because of our dedication to bettering their lives. In later chapters, we will examine the underlying cause of ADHD, the course of ADHD as children grow into adulthood, and the treatment of ADHD, which itself continues to grow and evolve.

EPIDEMIOLOGY

According to recent statistics from the United States Centers for Disease Control and Prevention, 7.8% of children (11% of boys, 4.4% of girls) aged four to seventeen years have been diagnosed with ADHD at some time in their lives. The most common form of ADHD is the combined type, in which children have symptoms of both inattention *and* hyperactivity-impulsivity. The predominantly inattentive type of ADHD is the next most common, in which children have only symptoms of inattention. These children have activity levels no different from those of children without ADHD, and they are no more talkative or impulsive than peers their age. The least common form of ADHD is the predominantly hyperactive-impulsive type, in which children are on the go, impulsive, talkative, and behaviorally disruptive but able to focus, listen, and follow directions equally well as peers their age.

ADHD is more common overall in boys than in girls. This may be because of higher rates of other behavioral problems (fighting, stealing, defiance of authority) in boys than in girls. It may be these other behavioral problems are more obvious or problematic and bring more boys to the attention of schools and doctors, thus increasing chances of ADHD diagnosis. A diagnosis of a behavioral problem such as oppositional defiant disorder (ODD) or conduct disorder (CD) may also lead to ADHD being uncovered and diagnosed. This leads to the apparently greater rate of ADHD in boys. ODD is present in the child who is extremely defiant to authority figures, whereas CD includes serious societal rule violations, such as theft or assault. These three "disruptive behavioral disorders" (ADHD, ODD, CD) often co-occur in one child.

Rates of ADHD are fairly consistent across a broad range of geographic, racial, and socioeconomic populations. As stated before, ADHD occurs in children outside the U.S. Recognition that ADHD occurs worldwide may increase treatment availability for children. Beginning early in the twenty-first century, international organizations, such as the World Health Organization, recognized ADHD as a worldwide concern, thereby aiding in the spread of knowledge and understanding. The public advocacy group, the World Federation for Mental Health, recently published guidelines declaring ADHD to be a "neurobiological disorder.... [whose] existence no longer should be debated."

Although ADHD is known to occur across the world, there are differences in reported rates between countries. These differences are most likely explained by varying definitions of ADHD used in different countries. For example, in studies using International Classification of Diseases criteria, rates may be lower because the criteria are more specific or restrictive. Conversely, whereas earlier *DSM* diagnostic criteria had a narrower focus based on hyperactivity, current criteria include hyperactive-impulsive and inattentive symptoms, resulting in higher rates of diagnosis.

It was once thought that ADHD was purely a childhood condition that did not persist into adulthood. Over the past five to ten years, the study of ADHD symptoms into adulthood has flourished, and the impact of ADHD in adulthood from a social-economic perspective is now appreciated to be significant. Approximately three quarters of children with ADHD will retain ADHD into adolescence, and approximately one half of adolescents will retain ADHD into adulthood. The current rates of ADHD in adulthood are estimated to be 4% to 5% of the U.S. adult population.

2

How Is ADHD Diagnosed?

THE CLINICAL HISTORY

The diagnosis of ADHD is made through a careful "clinical history." There is no blood test or brain x-ray to diagnose ADHD at this time. Therefore, the diagnosis is based on a *clinical* history, which means a doctor takes a verbal history from parents/guardians, from children themselves, and at times from other persons involved in the child's life such as a teacher or coach. The history involves standard questions about the presence of characteristic symptoms of this disorder (see the ADHD criteria in Chapter 1).

Pediatric or family practice doctors ("primary care doctors") are most often responsible for the diagnosis (and treatment) of ADHD because of the very limited supply of child and adolescent psychiatrists. In addition, pediatric neurologists, specialists in neurologic conditions in children like seizure disorders, commonly are asked by pediatricians to diagnose and treat children with ADHD. The role of pediatric neurology in the evaluation of this childhood disorder may be a result of limited psychiatry services. In addition, the role of pediatric neurology in the diagnosis may reflect the history of ADHD as a neurologic condition (i.e., "minimal brain dysfunction"), as discussed in Chapter 1. Finally, and unfortunately for some, there remains a discomfort, mistrust, and fear in using psychiatric services, specifically with children.

Child and adolescent psychiatrists are in short supply across the country, including in large metropolitan areas, although remote rural regions are particularly underserved. This leads to a difficult situation because the doctors (child and adolescent psychiatrists) who have the most behavioral training, the most in-depth experience with psychiatric medications, and, most critically, the time (because appointments are paid for by insurance) for management of conditions like ADHD are not the primary people assessing or treating these children.

At present day, there are approximately 7,000 child and adolescent psychiatrists in the U.S. Just as with any area of medicine, child psychiatrists have different areas of interest and experience. Some child and adolescent psychiatrists may be primarily therapists, not prescribing medications for conditions like ADHD. Child psychiatrists who do see children with ADHD may be more likely to see children with ADHD who have more complex problems, such as having ADHD and another psychiatric condition, like depression or an anxiety disorder, or children who have not responded to medications prescribed by a pediatrician or neurologist.

ADHD SYMPTOMS: THE KEY POINTS

To make a diagnosis based on a clinical interview, a doctor will begin by asking about the presence of ADHD symptoms: inattentiveness, distractibility, impulsivity, or hyperactivity (see Chapter 1). Discussions with the parent/guardian, child, and other individuals involved in the child's life may be part of the assessment. Each symptom must be considered carefully, following the key points outlined below.

The First Key Point

Each ADHD symptom must occur to a degree *that is unusual for a child his/her age*. Any child, particularly a young child aged six to seven years old, for example, will at times not listen, lose his/her items at school, or be hyperactive around the home. Children with ADHD stand apart from their peers by how often these symptoms happen (very much more) as compared with their peers.

For example, all children can at times not listen to their parents. Children with ADHD require repetition for them to listen, over and over and over again: "Did you hear me ... look at me ... put your listening ears on ... this is the tenth time I have asked you...." Parents, exasperated, can describe the majority of conversations to occur like that. Or, as another example, children with ADHD may lose items at school, and at home, on a *daily* basis. This may result in the purchase of several winter coats every winter, or multiple school texts or house keys; "He would lose his arm if it wasn't part of his body." Or, children with ADHD can be on the move "from the moment she wakes up, till she finally falls asleep exhausted." A coach may ask the child to quit the team because he never sits still when sent to the bench, or when out in the playing field the child may be running around all of the time, not with team. In all these examples, the child with ADHD has a common childhood symptom (not listening to a parent, losing an item, and being hyperactive) far more often than other children his/her age. These symptoms occur daily, often multiple times a day.

However, even though these symptoms happen much more often than with other children, sometimes adults will assume that the child is doing these things *on purpose*; he is not listening on purpose, he is losing items because he doesn't care, she is hyper because she wants to be. A teacher may say that "she is a sweet child, *not so interested in school . . .* but when she *sets her mind to a task, she can focus fine.*" The adult is assuming 1) that attention is under the child's control, and the child doesn't care or is lazy when not paying attention; and 2) that the child can't have ADHD because she can focus at specific times.

Responding to the first assumption (the child doesn't care about learning), it is safe to say that children, like adults, want to do well in what they are involved in. Although any child can find school boring at times, children do want to learn, succeed, and be proud of their accomplishments. The description of a child who "just is lazy or not interested" is an assumption, not a known fact. Instead, what the adult could say is "I *assume* she is not paying attention because she finds the class boring. . . ." Maybe instead, the child has ADHD, and, although she wants to pay attention, she can't help herself, drifting off during class, daydreaming about other things. Adults should be careful, and thoughtful, and not make conclusions until all the possible explanations are explored.

In responding to the second assumption (children who can pay attention at some times cannot have ADHD), children with ADHD can pay attention as well as their peers when something is very interesting, exciting, or ever-changing (e.g., TV, video games). We touched on this a bit in Chapter 1. A child with ADHD may seem to focus surprisingly well on TV or videos, which is so different from his/her inability to focus at other times. As another example, children with ADHD can pay attention when a parent/teacher gives them one-to-one assistance. In that case, the adult is greatly helping the child focus on a task by giving the child cues and encouragement. When left to do work by him/herself, the child with ADHD cannot focus, cannot ignore distractions, and cannot keep up with peers.

To summarize, the first key point is that for behaviors to be symptoms of ADHD, they must happen very often, which is *unusual for a child his/her age.*

If the behaviors happen that often, ADHD should be considered. Keep in mind, however, that there may be times when the child can focus and behave similarly to his/her peers, like when the child is focused on TV.

The Second Key Point

ADHD symptoms *must occur in more than one setting*. In other words, the child with ADHD has symptoms at school, in the home, and in other settings, such as during sports or music class. Any child can be restless or inattentive in just one setting, such as the child who doesn't focus well during one music lesson or one particularly difficult class. Instead, children with ADHD typically have symptoms and problems wherever they are.

However, as with any medical condition, some are "sicker" than others. Some children with ADHD are more symptomatic than others, such as those with a greater number of symptoms (eighteen as compared with six). Therefore, you can imagine that a child with severe (all eighteen) ADHD symptoms of hyperactivity-impulsivity and inattention-disorganization will appear different from his/her peers in any setting, at any time of day. These children can have problems in classrooms, birthday parties, family gatherings, cub scout meetings, anywhere and everywhere.

For other children with ADHD, the environment can play a role in how often symptoms of ADHD are noticed and how often they cause problems. Important environmental factors in school settings include the experience of the teacher, the size of the class, and the availability of resources, such as gymnasiums and playgrounds. A more experienced teacher, a smaller class size, and a huge outside play-space may all contribute to helping a child with ADHD manage in school. Important environmental aspects in home settings include the organization and health of the parents/guardians, the number of siblings, and the resources available to the family. A highly organized home, with no siblings and plenty of indoor and outdoor space to be active in, may all assist the child with ADHD to manage in the home.

It is also possible that a child's ADHD symptoms can cause greater problems in one setting than another, with more problems in a kindergarten classroom and less at home. At school, the child has great difficulty sitting for lessons with his classmates or standing in line for lunch, but while at home, the child is allowed to run around the yard, bounce endlessly on an indoor trampoline, and receive one-on-one supervision from a doting parent. Still, when looked at carefully, it should be clear that this child has symptoms of ADHD in more than one setting. He is nearly constantly on the go around the house. However, the home environment accommodates his activity level, and thus the problems are less conspicuous than at school.

It may be helpful to compare ADHD with other medical conditions to understand how much the environment can impact illnesses. For example, some children with asthma (difficulty breathing or wheezing) have more difficulty with breathing when exercising. If you take a child like that and allow him to only exercise once in a while, his asthma symptoms may not happen anymore, or just rarely. You have stopped the trigger, and taken the child from the situations that make the symptoms the worst.

To summarize, the second key point is that for behaviors to be symptoms of ADHD, they *must occur in more than one setting*. However, depending on the child and the setting, these symptoms may cause more or less problems. Just because a parent has *allowed* a child to be hyperactive about the house doesn't mean that the child is acting normally, like his/her peers.

The Third Key Point

ADHD symptoms must *be present before age seven*. Historically, ADHD has been seen as a childhood disorder. Consistent with this, parents will describe children with ADHD as being on the move from early infancy; "She never walked, she went from crawling to running." Hyperactivity may be most obvious when the child is faced with greater expectations, such as sitting for circle time in kindergarten, at age five to six. Suddenly, it may become quite evident that this child is unusually hyperactive in comparison with his/her peers (first and second key points).

However, for some, symptoms may not come to the attention of teachers, parents, and doctors until later in adolescence. Yet still, with careful questioning, ADHD symptoms typically can be identified in past years, back to before age seven. The parent may say, "He has always been really active" or "We have always had to help more with organization and routines around the house." Although these symptoms happened more than with other children, it didn't seem like they caused the same degree of problems in all settings, until the academic demands adolescents face overwhelmed the teen's ability to manage.

In the study of the course of ADHD, some researchers are questioning whether age matters in the diagnosis. For any given child, symptoms may be most problematic at age five, six, seven, eight, nine, ten, and so on. It makes sense that a problem with attention and activity level would be present throughout ones' life but may vary in its impact at a given age.

Scientific challenge: Is a specific age of onset of symptoms important in the diagnosis of ADHD? How would you determine that?

Interview one hundred adults who have current ADHD symptoms and ask them what the "age of onset" of their symptoms/problems was. At what age were the symptoms of ADHD 1) unusual as compared with peers, 2) evident in more than one setting, and 3) causing problems? The majority of adults with ADHD will be able to describe symptoms and problems back to kindergarten, ages five to seven. However, some adults may report symptoms starting at ages twelve to thirteen, when they entered middle school, a time when they were asked to change classes (not be in one room all day), had more work to do, and faced new challenges of a large, complex school building.

Now, compare these two groups of adults, those with ADHD symptoms before age seven and those with symptoms that began closer to age twelve. Are they more similar than different? Are the symptoms similar, did the symptoms happen in multiple settings, and have the symptoms continued on into adulthood? Does each group have a lot of other family members with ADHD? Does each group respond the same way to medications?

Based upon current research, it appears the answer to these questions may be yes. Adults with onset at six or thirteen appear more similar than different. Does that convince you that an exact age of onset in childhood does not matter? Should this research be enough to change the way ADHD is diagnosed in this country? Meaning that the third key point above would change from "symptoms of ADHD must *be present before age seven*" to something like "symptoms of ADHD must *be present beginning in childhood*." We will revisit this issue when discussing the research on adult ADHD later in the book.

To summarize, at present, the third key point is that for behaviors to be symptoms of ADHD, they *must be present before age seven*. Whether this will change in the future remains to be seen.

The Fourth Key Point

ADHD symptoms *should not be explained by another condition*. This is the same for any medical-psychiatric diagnosis. In other words, ADHD should not be diagnosed in a child who, on the basis of a thorough clinical history, has another condition that better explains the symptoms. To come to this conclusion, the doctor will consider other factors that may play a role in the child's health. This is done most effectively by knowing the child/family over time and assessing "biological factors," "psychological factors," and "social factors." Biological factors may include having a medical illness or drug addiction that explains why the child is not paying attention. Psychological factors may include symptoms of anxiety and depression. Social factors may include personal or family stressors, such as a family death or divorce.

As an example, a parent might bring her daughter to the doctor with concerns that she does not pay attention in class. It turns out that this child has daily anxiety; she doesn't pay attention in class because of her panic that she may be called upon, and, in addition, her beloved grandmother died last month, and she is sadly thinking of her grandmother in class. She is eleven years old, and there has been no concern about ADHD in the past school years, nor have there been any problems with paying attention in other places, such as home or dance class. The conclusion is that her symptoms result from a combination of grief and anxiety and not ADHD.

To summarize, for a child to receive the diagnosis of ADHD, multiple key points must be considered when taking a clinical history. Behaviors must be 1) *unusual for a child his/her age*, 2) *present in more than one setting*, 3) *present before age seven*, and 4) *not explained by another condition*.

SCREENING OR RATING SCALES

In addition to the clinical history, to make the diagnosis of ADHD, some doctors, schools, and families will use rating scales. These are usually pencil-paper forms that list symptoms of ADHD (and at times ask about symptoms that may or may not accompany ADHD, like moodiness, low self-esteem, defiance). The ratings can be tallied to estimate whether ADHD is likely in the child being rated or determine the severity of the ADHD symptoms.

Rating scales are available in assessing a child's behavior in home and at school. Often, parents will complete a scale to rate ADHD symptoms at home, a teacher will rate the same child's symptoms in the classroom, and the doctor will review all the materials together to consider the diagnosis of ADHD. These scales can be helpful, but they are not necessary, and they should not take the place of a clinical history taken by a doctor.

COGNITIVE TESTING

People like to have "objective evidence" (seen by others) of ADHD. However, at present, there is no paper-pencil test to diagnose ADHD. "Neuropsychological testing" or "cognitive testing" includes tests to assess intelligence, reading, math skills, as well as emotional health. Parents may be confused hearing that their child has problems in school and needs "testing" to determine the problem. As we discussed before, a child who is failing in school deserves a careful assessment; however, there are different assessments for different problems.

For the child who is struggling only in math class and not in any other class, educational testing is appropriate and may identify a specific math disability, a specific learning problem. Learning disorders often occur in children who also have ADHD. Testing can be helpful to identify learning problems, including in children with ADHD. However, cognitive testing is not needed for a child who is inattentive, distracted, disorganized, and making careless mistakes in all classes, yet who clearly gets the material when a teacher sits down with him one-to-one. This sounds more like ADHD than a specific learning disability. The child and parents should meet with a doctor to have a clinical interview, considering ADHD as the diagnosis.

In addition, the *absence* of attention problems in cognitive testing does not mean that the child does not have ADHD. Sitting down to new, interesting cognitive tasks in a small, quiet room with a friendly examiner can allow children with ADHD to appear quite "normal." The typical struggles of inattention, distractibility, and disorganization may not be observed in this artificial (not like real classroom life) setting. The examiner and parents might make the mistake of concluding that it can't be ADHD.

To make a comparison with asthma, as we did before, to decide a child does not have ADHD based on observing a child during one test would be similar to saying, "Well, the child isn't wheezing *right now* in my office, so it must not be asthma." Testing is like taking one picture of a child. To make an ADHD diagnosis, one needs a video tape of the child. That video tape, so to speak, is obtained through a clinical history, asking questions about how the child performs day to day and not just at one moment in time.

EXECUTIVE FUNCTIONING

Science continues to search for objective measures of ADHD and cognitive problems that can be found alongside ADHD. There may be a certain group of children, teens, and adults with ADHD who have greater difficulty with "executive functioning." Executive functioning refers to organizational abilities, planning, memory, and prioritizing. To have trouble with executive functioning (dysfunctioning) is like having a bad boss running a company. If the boss or chief executive is not organized, is not prepared for meetings, is late is not able to shift priorities, and has no sense of direction for the company, the company may not survive.

Individuals with ADHD who have executive dysfunctioning struggle more with organizational aspects of their lives than do others. These persons can be much more impaired in how they function day to day, month to month, and year to year, whether in school or at work or at home. Scientists are searching for ways of identifying individuals with executive dysfunction. Cognitive testing may be helpful, although as stated before, it may be helpful if the problems are identified during testing.

PSYCHIATRIC COMORBIDITY

Any child brought to a doctor for concerns associated with school or social functioning should be assessed for a host of psychiatric conditions because ADHD is often accompanied by one or more other mental health problems. We call these "psychiatric comorbidities," meaning co-occurring problems. In addition to ADHD, common areas assessed include mood symptoms (sadness, anger/irritability, euphoria), anxiety symptoms (social fears, anxiety attacks, generalized fears, obsessions, compulsions), disruptive behaviors (defiance, stealing, lying), substance misuse (alcohol, marijuana), and eating disorders (intentional weight loss).

In asking about these symptoms it is best to consider each as a possible distinct, individual problem. For example, although many children with ADHD can be discouraged about their school and peer problems, sadness is typically short-lived, mild, and a result of their academic struggles. However, there are other kinds of sadness, which we call major depression or dysthymia. Major depression is sadness that is pervasive, meaning sadness that occurs in other places besides school, and is accompanied by sleep, eating, and energy problems. In addition, major depression can include low interest, guilt, hopelessness, and thoughts of suicide. Dysthymia is more of a chronic, milder form of depression but still certainly can interfere with a person's functioning.

Similarly, a child with ADHD may be anxious or worried about forgetting objects or losing items of personal importance. However, a child with ADHD who has worries that extend to non-ADHD related issues, such as health or money, and who has other symptoms like body tension, sleep problems, and irritability may have a comorbid anxiety disorder like generalized anxiety disorder.

It is very important to ask about other psychiatric problems in diagnosing and treating children with ADHD. One can expect an increased chance of other psychiatric problems just because the child has ADHD. It is also important to realize that these other psychiatric problems may appear at other times during a child's development. For example, some disorders, especially drug and alcohol addictions, can begin to emerge once the child enters adolescence.

PHYSICAL EXAMINATION

Physical examinations can be used in the evaluation for ADHD, but there is no expectation that ADHD can be determined based upon physical findings. However, children with ADHD can have other medical conditions, which can be diagnosed by physical examination, and therefore it is up to the doctor to determine what physical examinations or medical assessments are appropriate during the evaluation of a child with ADHD.

In those children with a sudden onset of ADHD symptoms, a physical examination can be used to look for another medical-physical condition, such as a brain injury. ADHD-like symptoms have been described as the most common new difficulties that follow traumatic brain injury in children. In a child with a history of difficulty with attention after an accident, like a car accident, a doctor may order an x-ray (computed tomography scan, magnetic resonance imagery scan) of the brain to look for an injured area. Or, a test may be conducted to look for abnormal electrical activity (*seizure* activity) in the brain (electroencephalogram, or EEG).

ADHD TREATMENT: SUPPORTING THE DIAGNOSIS

As with other areas of medicine, after a child is diagnosed with ADHD, the treatment of ADHD should back up the diagnosis. In other words, ADHD treatment should result in significant improvement of the child's symptoms and overall functioning to meet or approach the level of symptoms and functioning of children his/her age. Generally speaking, ADHD treatments are very effective and specific. Approximately 75% of children will respond to a medication, often times the first medication, and the response is a specific improvement in ADHD symptoms.

Although we would like all medical diagnoses to be 100% certain, this is not the case, of course. Therefore, the practice of medicine involves assessment and reassessment over time. Doctors form best "hypotheses" based on clinical interviews, and, in some areas of medicine, blood tests or imaging tests. Doctors then use a combination of treatment and further assessments to come to conclusions. As an example outside the context of ADHD, if a doctor expects a child's cough to be caused by an infection and treatment with an antibiotic doesn't result in a cure, then the doctor should consider other possible causes of the cough. If the child with an ADHD diagnosis does not respond to ADHD medications, then the diagnosis of ADHD should be reconsidered.

A CASE EXAMPLE OF A YOUNG CHILD WITH ADHD

What follows is a "case" example of a child with ADHD, taking the above clinical history approach. The case is meant to illustrate the type of very specific information gathered during an assessment of a child for ADHD. This child is a fictional child, based upon histories taken in the diagnosis of many children with ADHD. The history is taken from a mom, a dad, and a child named "John" during a 90-minute office appointment. Mom and Dad provide reports from school and from other settings.

John is a six-year-old boy who comes to the office with his mother and father because of concerns voiced in school. Mom and Dad describe John as a healthy, "usually" good-tempered boy, who has been increasingly disruptive in school. John is in first grade in a local public elementary school. Although last year his kindergarten teacher reported he was "quite an active rambunctious boy," John had only ten children in his class that year, and his school day was only four hours long (some school systems have only half-day kindergarten). This year, first grade, John's class has twenty-four children and lasts a full day, from 9 AM to 3 PM.

John's teacher, "Mrs. F," tells Mom and Dad that he is "constantly" on the move in the classroom, climbing about his seat, turning around, tying his shoe, getting a drink of water, going to the restroom, and getting a tissue. In addition, he talks to his peers, shouts out answers, and "barges in on other children quietly playing." John is not able to entertain himself, quietly, for more than five to ten minutes. He is unable to stand in line to go to lunch, and he bumps into others, gets out of line, or tries to jump up and touch banners hanging overhead in the hallway.

At recess John is now asked to stay nearby the teachers and is not allowed to use the jungle-gym. Although the school year is only two months along, he has been sent to the school nurse four times for mild injuries; examples include leaping off the top of the structure, and running too fast around a corner without looking.

Mrs. F states clearly that these symptoms occur every day, in and out of the classroom; are causing problems for him and the others in his class; and are quite unusual as compared with his peers. In addition, she is concerned that John is unable to stick with an activity, like a writing lesson. He becomes off task, "almost immediately," and if not, is typically so quick with his work that he makes careless mistakes. Mrs. F knows John is intelligent because at times, when very interested, he can contribute to class discussions with excellent vocabulary and understanding. As is well-known by Mom/Dad, his backpack "is like a tornado that has touched down" with papers and lunch scattered throughout. Either Mom/Dad or Mrs. F regularly remind John to grab his coat and gloves before leaving the classroom at the end of day, or he seems to "totally forget, as if I never reminded him."

Around the house, Mom/Dad describe John as a very active boy, who they keep a close eye on. They are concerned he may seriously injure himself because he seems "reckless" riding his bike into the street without looking or climbing too high in trees. He will often leap down the stairs or jump off his bed; "We always know where he is, he is never playing quietly by himself." He does not sit, but instead stands for meals or "uses the chair as some sort of play equipment."

In addition, Mom and Dad become quite frustrated that they must repeat directions to him "a million times." At times they will take his hand to physically lead him through evening routines. For example, if they were to ask John to "go to your room and get into your pajamas," within minutes they will find him playing in the study. When confronted, he often looks up with surprise and then says, "Woops, sorry, I forgot." He had been fully intending to go to his room but a toy caught his eye (distracted, off task) and the parents' request was immediately forgotten.

Finally, when asked about other places and activities that have been a problem, Mom/Dad admit that they don't take him to as many places as they would like, for fear of injury (the grocery store parking lot), peer rejection (too hyperactive and not listening; at a recent birthday party, asked to leave), or family rejection (last holiday party, he broke a precious heirloom by accident, running too fast in his grandparents' small house).

Based upon this history, John meets almost all of the criteria for ADHD, combined type. He has multiple (>6) symptoms of inattention and hyperactivity-impulsivity, beginning at an early age, unusual compared with his peers, and appearing in multiple settings. However, are there other factors (biological, psychological, social) that could explain John's symptoms?

John lives at home with his parents and his four-month-old sibling. Mom works part-time for dad's sales company. Dad works full-time but is home most nights and weekends. They have lived in the community for years and have supportive friends and relatives. John does not have any physical health concerns, and he takes no medications. There have been no serious health concerns for the rest of the family, nor personal stressors. A cousin on mom's side of the family has been diagnosed with ADHD, and dad is pretty convinced, in talking about his son's symptoms, that he had some similar problems as a child, though not as severe. As will be discussed, ADHD runs in families, which implies abnormal genes being passed from father or mother to son. There are no obvious psychological factors; John is a boy without significant mood or anxiety problems. Despite his ADHD symptoms, he is generally happy and well liked. However, there are some signs that this is changing, with John's report of having fewer friends and feeling bad about being spoken to for "bad behavior."

Based upon this additional information, John meets the criteria for ADHD, combined type. This combination of daily symptoms are very unusual as compared with other boys his age, they are present in most if not all places where he goes, they are present in early childhood, before age seven, and there is no other reasonable explanation or other condition to explain their presence.

A CASE EXAMPLE OF AN ADOLESCENT WITH ADHD

What follows is a "case" example of a teenager with ADHD, taking a similar clinical history approach. This teen is fictional, based upon histories taken in the diagnosis of many adolescents with ADHD. The history is taken from a single mom and a girl named "Cindy" during a 90-minute office appointment. Mom provides reports from school and from other settings.

Cindy is a fifteen-year-old girl who comes to the office with her mother because of concerns voiced by Mom that she is "going to be kicked out of school." Mom describes Cindy as a healthy, happy younger child, who has been increasingly in trouble at home, socially, and in school. Cindy is in ninth grade in a local regional high school. Cindy "was a pleasure" during elementary school years, never in trouble, and "just a sweet, good kid." This year, Cindy has entered a large regional high school as a ninth grader.

One of Mom's complaints is that she cannot get any information from school about how Cindy is doing, and just recently, a midterm report card came out with Cs and one D, her lowest grades ever. In elementary school and middle school she was a B student, with an occasional A "when she really liked it." The few notes from school cite missing homework and inconsistent test grades. Cindy also recently had a suspension when she was found out of school, in the area behind the school with a group of older teens, where all were smoking cigarettes.

In talking about Cindy as a younger child, mom recalls wondering if she was really listening to her often. She felt she needed to repeat directions to her "over and over, like, 'hey, Cindy, I need your eyes to me now!'" She developed the practice of giving her almost one-word directions, like "pajamas, teeth, bed." Yet, she would still become off task and not complete these routines. Very often she would forget things that mom had asked her to do, "so I really don't ask her to remember much, I step in for her." This applies to organizational issues as well; mom just rolls her eyes when asked if Cindy manages her time or organizes herself.

Although mom initially says that no teacher complained about these issues, she then says on further reflection that "of course, everyone would say she can be 'spacey,' but she was such a sweet girl." So, teachers would place her at the front of the class, check in with her, remind her, locate pens for her, and the like. And mom would do the same around the home. In other settings, Cindy had some struggles with organized activities as well. As a younger child, mom was her assistant gymnastic coach. "I volunteered so that she could make it, otherwise they were going to ask her to leave." Cindy at first wasn't listening to her coaches and was not practicing the requested moves.

Coming back to present, mom says Cindy was "just frankly lost" when she entered this high school year. Mom is no longer able to monitor her academics, given all the different teachers and classes. She doesn't seem able to study in the afternoon, appears to never know when tests are, and her grades continue to decline. In addition, she has become increasingly defiant, and irritable when asked to help out about the home. She "makes bad decisions" such as smoking and cutting classes, new behaviors this past month.

Based upon this history, Cindy meets the criteria for ADHD, inattentive type. She has multiple symptoms of inattention, beginning at an early age, unusual compared with her peers, and appearing in multiple settings. Although these issues didn't in the past have the same impact on her grades as they do currently, the symptoms of ADHD were present. However, are there other factors (biological, psychological, social) that could explain Cindy's symptoms?

Cindy lives at home with her mom. Mom works full-time, but is able to be home at dinner. They have lived in the same home for years and have supportive extended family in the area. Cindy has no physical health concerns and takes no medications. There are several relatives with ADHD known to mom.

Recently, Cindy feels that she has lost many of her old friends, with whom she doesn't share classes in her current "huge, massive school." This is a significant stressor for her. Overall, despite the stressors in Cindy's life, she remains interested in changing course with her academics, wants to "start the year over," and becomes teary when admitting she has been smoking after school. "It's something to do, stupid, I know."

Based upon this additional information, Cindy still meets the criteria for ADHD, inattentive type. There is no other reasonable explanation or other condition to explain the symptoms' presence. In addition, these symptoms are lifelong and cause more problems than in others. It seems that her acting out, skipping class, smoking, and being defiant can be understood as reactions to doing poorly in school, which can be traced back to the significant ADHD symptoms.

In closing, these cases of a child and an adolescent with ADHD are representative of typical symptoms in each age group. At the conclusion of each evaluation session, everyone (child/teen/parent) is educated about ADHD and its impact. The conversation then turns to treatment. Although all of these families are interested in treatments for ADHD, they want to understand more about the causes of the disorder first. So, let's turn our attention to that topic.

3

How Does a Child Get ADHD?

ADHD most likely results from a variety of sources, including genes and the environment. Genes are made of DNA; DNA provides the "codes" for all aspects of human behavior. DNA can include codes for disorders as well, such as ADHD or cancer. Genes may influence how a body responds to an environmental stress, which in turn leads to a disorder. The end result may be specific damage to nerve cells in a brain area and abnormal brain functioning. We do not currently know exactly how an individual child develops ADHD. We cannot point to one gene, or one environmental moment, and say "that caused ADHD."

Therefore, in this chapter, we will discuss the *risk* for ADHD, given the *influence* of genes and the *influence* of the environment. Because we do not know the exact cause, we cannot talk about the *cause* of ADHD, only *risk factors*, which may increase the likelihood of having ADHD. We will also discuss environmental factors that do not appear to directly increase the risk for ADHD.

INCREASED RISK FOR ADHD BASED ON FAMILY HISTORY

We do know that ADHD runs in families at an unusually high rate. A child with ADHD is more likely to have a relative with ADHD than another child who does not have ADHD. A disorder that runs in families (occurs in a number of family members across generations) likely involves gene(s) passed down through generations.

The first step of genetic investigation is to conduct family studies of ADHD, to demonstrate that ADHD runs in families. These studies involve careful assessments of multiple members of a given family, across generations, to make the diagnosis of ADHD and other medical or psychiatric conditions. In families of children *with ADHD*, it is *very common* to have a "first-degree" relative (parent, sibling) with ADHD as well. In families of children *without ADHD*, it is *less common* to have a first-degree relative (parents, siblings) with ADHD. Similarly, adults with ADHD very often have children with ADHD as compared with adults who do not have ADHD.

Scientific challenge: Do high rates of ADHD in families mean ADHD is genetic? Could ADHD rather result from the way the children are raised? One could argue that high rates of ADHD in families are just the result of having a disorganized parent with ADHD who passes that disorganization on to a child and increases his/her ADHD risk.

So, to investigate this, examine the biological siblings (same parents; shared genes) and adopted siblings (no shared genes) of children with ADHD. Examine and compare the rates of ADHD in all the children. Biological relatives of children with ADHD are *more likely* to have ADHD than are adopted family members of these children. If ADHD was caused by a disorganized family environment, all persons who live in the same environment would have similar rates of ADHD. In studies, very high rates of ADHD are found in biological twins, that is, children who share genetic makeup.

Current studies find that ADHD is one of the most heritable (passed down in families) of psychiatric disorders. When thinking about the chances of a child having ADHD, one could say that approximately 75% to 80% of this chance is the result of genes. What about genetic studies, then?

INCREASED RISK FOR ADHD BASED ON GENETIC STUDIES

The gene(s) responsible for ADHD are still unknown. To find the answers to the question "Where does ADHD come from?" current researchers draw blood samples from children and adults with ADHD for genetic testing. The blood sample is used to extract DNA for genetic studies.

It is likely that the genes responsible for ADHD are the ones involved in controlling how chemical messages are passed between specific areas of the brain. If a gene responsible for forming a receiving unit (receptor) on a nerve cell is abnormal, then the receptor may not function properly. If the receptor is not functioning normally, the chemical message between nerve cells is not effective, and the brain area will not function normally.

It is likely that a combination of several genes, perhaps a different combination for different people, results in ADHD. Genes suspected as involved in ADHD include genes that code for chemical transporters (dopamine transporters, or the "DAT" gene) and genes for a specific chemical receptor type (dopamine receptor, or "DRD4"). To determine which abnormal gene(s) cause ADHD, very large numbers of blood samples are needed; research on this area is underway in this country and abroad. At the close of this book, we will discuss the latest in genetic studies of ADHD.

On a side note, genetic studies also include investigations of genes involved in a body's response to a medication, including ADHD medications. First, some background: a body's typical response to a swallowed medication is to 1) absorb it into the bloodstream; 2) metabolize it, that is, break down the chemical in to smaller parts to allow it to work; and then allow for 3) elimination, such as in the urine. Elimination ends the effect of the medication.

Genes can play an important role in this process. Genes can cause rapid metabolism of medication (the body breaks down medications quickly), and genes can cause slow metabolism (the body breaks down medications slowly). Therefore, a person who is a rapid metabolizer might feel little effect, good or bad, from a typical dose of a medication because his/her body breaks it down so quickly. Conversely, a person who is a slow metabolizer might feel excess effect from the same medication, such as an unusual amount of side effects, because of his/her body's very slow breakdown and elimination of the medication.

INCREASED RISK FOR ADHD BASED ON THE ENVIRONMENT

In addition to genes that are passed down through families, events in the environment can also increase a child's risk of having ADHD. Influences on a child can occur at the earliest stages of brain development, during pregnancy, or later on during childhood.

Pregnancy and Delivery Complications

Environmental risk factors for ADHD include events that happen during pregnancy. During pregnancy, multiple situations could reduce the delivery of critically needed blood, oxygen, and nutrients to the developing fetus. Such limitations in vital resources could directly affect the development of the brain and increase the risk of that child developing ADHD. Specific parts of the brain may be affected; some brain areas are more vulnerable (easily damaged) than others.

Sadly, in the United States, it is still common for women to drink alcohol and to smoke cigarettes during pregnancy. These exposures in pregnancy may increase the risk of a child having ADHD. Fetal alcohol syndrome (FAS) is a childhood syndrome that can be caused by a mother drinking too much alcohol in pregnancy. FAS effects include mental retardation, abnormal-appearing facial features, and a small head size. ADHD-like behaviors, such as hyperactivity and problems with learning and memory, language, attention, organization, as well as social skills, have been observed in children with exposure to alcohol during pregnancy.

Studies have shown that tobacco smoking during pregnancy reduces growth of the fetus and also may have a negative impact on brain development and behavior. Some studies have shown that mothers who smoke during pregnancy may double the risk of having a child with ADHD. Tobacco smoke can cause growth problems because of the change in normal blood flow to the fetus, reducing nutrition as well as bringing toxins to the brain (the ingredients in cigarettes). Nicotine, the chemical in cigarettes, may directly cause lower activity of certain chemical systems (dopamine) in the developing brain. This makes sense if we remember that stimulant medications, the treatment for ADHD, increase the dopamine message in the brain.

Environment: Exposure to Toxins

The toxin lead has been shown to cause symptoms of ADHD: distractibility, hyperactivity, and lower intellectual functioning. Lead can be found in paint from old homes and can be swallowed by young children by accident during play in the home. However, the majority of children with ADHD do not have lead contamination, and many children who have had high lead exposure have not developed ADHD. So, as mentioned before, lead exposure may be a risk factor but is not *the cause* of ADHD.

Other toxins, such as mercury, manganese, and polychlorinated biphenyls, have been considered related to the development of ADHD. Children can be exposed to excess toxins through food; chemicals once used in the U.S. for paints and other manufacturing may be encountered by way of unintentional entry into the food chain as well. Chemicals from plants can enter the soil and water, eventually contaminating food supplies. Exposure to these toxins has been at times associated with such ADHD symptoms as inattention in children and hyperactivity in research animals.

Despite claims that ADHD is caused by certain types of foods or additives, and therefore that ADHD can be cured by a change in the diet, there is no firm scientific evidence that this is true.

Environment: Social or Psychological Stressors

To no surprise, the study of social or psychological stressors has demonstrated that children with a collection of such risk factors have an increased likelihood of emotional problems. Risk factors may include severe conflict between parents, poverty/lower social class, large family size, and emotional problems or criminal behavior in the parents. Trauma to children also increases general risk of emotional disturbance, including symptoms of ADHD. Traumatized children can have problems with lack of concentration, impulsivity and hyperactivity, or increased response to the environment.

Environment: The Powers of Television

TV viewing has been associated with emotional problems in children. More hours of TV watching have been *associated* with attention problems, aggression, and behavioral problems. However, associations of TV viewing with ADHD do not mean that TV causes ADHD.

Researchers have tried to figure out whether TV does cause higher rates of ADHD. The difficulty is that higher rates of TV watching in young children may be found in certain families for many reasons. It may be that other issues associated with these families are the actual reason why the risk of ADHD is increased and TV watching is just a symptom of these issues. For example, it may be that families with lower incomes, less child care services, and less space to play in the home may place children in front of the TV out of necessity, as compared with families with higher incomes and services/activities available to them. Also, it may be that less access to medical care and care during pregnancy for lower-income families results in higher-risk pregnancies, with more complications. Therefore, it is the birth complications in these families that are directly responsible for the increased risk for ADHD, not the low income and not the TV viewing.

"G × E": GENES × ENVIRONMENT

The combination of genes and the environment may provide the best explanation for how a child develops ADHD. For example, in a study of the influence of smoking during pregnancy and ADHD, the diagnosis of ADHD was greater in twins who had inherited a specific gene *and* who had exposure to smoke during pregnancy. Similar studies have been done with specific genes *and* excess alcohol use during pregnancy, which lead to increased ADHD diagnoses.

If "G × E" interactions are the cause of ADHD, the very wide range of possible combinations of genetic factors and environmental factors may explain why it is so difficult to find the "true cause" of ADHD. The goal in determining the cause(s) is to reduce the risk of ADHD. It might be that, by making changes in the environment for certain children with the ADHD genes, you could reduce or prevent ADHD.

Brain Abnormalities in ADHD

In ADHD, brain dysfunction may be caused by "top-down" problems with control of behavior and thinking. In ADHD, the top (front) part of the brain is not managing or controlling the rest of the brain. To function "normally," the brain must allow for one action or thought and at the same time prevent other actions or thoughts from interfering. The brain must help to process important information that we are focused upon (reading this book), but it must also help us to ignore other information around us (the sound of a car driving by, the drip of a faucet) that is not important when the task at hand is to read this book. In another example, someone driving a car must be able to maintain attention to the road in front of him/her while ignoring the conversations occurring in the back seat or a car horn honking on another street.

As will be discussed in a later chapter, brain areas function with the activity of certain brain chemicals, messengers that are called neurotransmitters. The neurotransmitters involved in ADHD are dopamine and norepinephrine. Researchers working on ADHD came to understand the importance of these chemicals by working backward. Take benzedrine (the arithmetic pill described in Chapter 1), for example. Understanding that a stimulant medication increases the dopamine chemical signal between nerve cells and that children respond with improved focus and behavior leads one to hypothesize that ADHD must be caused by an abnormal dopamine signal. In other words, 1) the amount of dopamine may be abnormally low in persons with ADHD, or 2) the dopamine message may not be normally received by the adjacent nerve cell, despite a normal amount of dopamine.

Scientists across the country and the world are studying the brains of children and adults with ADHD, making comparisons with "healthy" subjects without ADHD to determine the specific abnormal brain structures (their size) and specific abnormal brain activity (their function) of ADHD. It remains uncertain as to whether the influence of specific abnormal genes or specific environmental stressors will be able to be seen on brain imaging. Although medical technology has advanced in a remarkable fashion, brain abnormalities that cause ADHD may still not be seen even with our finest pictures.

To summarize, at present, we do not know the cause of ADHD. We cannot attribute one or two causes for an individual child. However, we can say that the combination of abnormal genes and environmental stressors is most likely working together to result in a child having ADHD. A child's brain may start out abnormally formed because of the influence of genes and may then be additionally influenced (damaged) by an environmental insult, such as tobacco smoking by the mother during pregnancy. Overall, the child's brain may be slow to mature and develop, and may never reach the same size/function as that of a "healthy" child. The brain may then be influenced in a positive or negative manner by later attempts at treatment, such as medications.

4

The Process of Drug Development

WHY TALK ABOUT DRUG DEVELOPMENT?

The model of psychiatric treatment is an integrated model, combining biological treatment (medications), psychological treatment (therapy), and social supports and treatments. For ADHD, biological treatment principally involves medications, mainly the stimulant-type medications. Psychological treatment may involve therapy for the child and/or family, addressing self-esteem issues and social and family conflicts. Social treatments can include social support groups for the child, increasing social connections in and out of school, as well as social supports for the family and the location of community resources.

To understand the complex issues involved in medications for children with ADHD, it is quite helpful to know something about the drug development process. In so doing, you can realize both the strengths of gathering information on how children respond to ADHD medications as well as the limitations of this process.

DRUG DEVELOPMENT: A HISTORICAL VIEWPOINT

Historically speaking, drugs have been used in children without the same level of study as drugs for adults. Remarkably, in this twenty-first century, new laws are still being formed to address this problem. The goal is to properly evaluate a new drug for use in children from the beginning of the drug's discovery, even when the drug is being developed for adult use. For example, a new drug being developed by a drug company ("pharmaceutical company") for adult asthma should include studies of the drug in children. The government is committed to obtaining data on the safety and effectiveness of drugs in large, highly monitored groups of children from the beginning of a drug's life and making this data available to the public.

To grasp the necessity of this, it is important to understand that once a drug is approved for a specific age group for a specific condition by the U.S. Food and Drug Administration (FDA; see below), it becomes available for widespread use. Doctors can prescribe and study the new drug in other age groups. Doctors who treat children may prescribe a new "adult drug" to their patients to see if it works for children as well. Doctors can study the new drug for other conditions as well, such as in the study of benzedrine, as described in Chapter 1.

Generally speaking, this process of study of a new drug can lead to important discoveries: that the drug works well in children, or that the drug works well for other conditions. Having pediatric safety and effectiveness data from the beginning of a drug's life allows this research process to proceed in a safe and appropriate manner.

DRUG DEVELOPMENT: THE PROCESS

Drug development can span decades. The process involves careful examination of 1) how safe the drug is and 2) how effective the drug is. At a basic science level, scientists first examine the chemical itself, in a laboratory, and examine the effect and safety of the chemical when given to animals. The government has developed specific rules about the current use of animals in drug development. The process of drug development then follows a series of specific steps or "phases" after the remarkably painstaking, complex process of basic science laboratory research. The process involves clinical trials, the phases of which will be discussed in detail in this chapter.

In the first phase (phase I) of human clinical trials, the experimental chemical, now given a drug name, is tested in a small group of people for the first time. The purpose of this first step is to evaluate safety, determine doses of the drug to be used, and identify side effects. In phase II, the drug is studied in a larger group of people, again to assess efficacy and safety. Phase III involves study of the drug in much larger groups of people (hundreds, thousands). The purpose of this phase is to confirm the effectiveness of the drug and monitor for side effects in the specific group of people it has been developed for. The drug can also be compared with other commonly used, previously FDA approved treatments.

Pharmaceutical companies are typically the ones to support this drug development effort, spending hundreds of millions of dollars investigating and developing a drug, leading to a massive report submitted to the U.S. FDA (see below). Once the U.S. FDA approves the drug, the company can sell it, in person or by ads on the TV or radio or newspaper, for the specific age and specific condition for which it is approved. But again, once the drug is approved, it enters the marketplace and can be used by others, with other ages, and with other conditions.

CLINICAL TRIALS: THE DETAILS

Carefully conducted clinical trials are the fastest and safest way to find treatments that work in people and that improve health. In a clinical trial, people (children, adults) are given a medication and are carefully assessed over a period of time to determine the effect and the safety of the medication.

Clinical trials can be developed and funded by a variety of organizations or individuals, including doctors, medical institutions, foundations, pharmaceutical companies, and many federal agencies, such as the National Institutes of Health (NIH), the Department of Defense (DOD), and the Department of Veteran's Affairs (VA). Clinical trials can take place in a variety of locations: hospitals, doctors' offices, and community clinics. However, it is law that all institutions that conduct clinical research with humans must have a review board, an Institutional Review Board (IRB), which approves and reviews research. An IRB is an independent committee of physicians, nurses, other scientists, and community advocates. The IRB makes certain that a clinical trial is ethical and the rights of study participants (human volunteers) are protected.

For a person to decide whether to participate in a clinical trial, the purpose, procedures, risks, and benefits must all be spelled out clearly and consent must be granted by that person. In addition, the consent states that participation is confidential (a person's name is not made public) and voluntary. A "consent form" outlines all of the following details:

- What is the purpose of the study?
- Who is going to be in the study?
- Why do researchers believe the treatment may be effective?
- Has it been tested before?
- What kinds of tests and experimental treatments are involved?

- Who will be in charge of my care?
- How will I know that the experimental treatment is working?
- How long will the trial last?
- What are the possible risks, side effects, and benefits in the study?
- Who will pay for the experimental treatment?
- Will I be reimbursed for other expenses?
- What type of follow-up care is part of this study?
- Will results of the trials be provided to me?

In clinical studies of children, special precautions are additionally made. Children are involved in the consent process and typically will be asked to sign an "assent form," which reviews the information in the parent's consent form but in appropriate language that a child can understand. Therefore, participation of a child in a clinical trial involves the review and signing of a consent form with the child's parent(s) or guardian(s) and review and signing of an assent form with the child participant.

A clinical trial designed to study a new or existing medication typically involves several important features, as identified in the name "*double-blind, placebo-controlled, randomized clinical trial* of medication x in children and adolescents with ADHD." The first feature is "*double blind*," which means both the doctor and the subject are "blinded." In the study, a child can receive one of two "medications" (as discussed next). Neither the doctor nor the child/subject knows which medication is received. In this way, no one is biased. If the doctor or subject knew what they were receiving, either might be more likely to say that it works.

Clinical trials are often also "*placebo controlled*." A placebo is an inactive, pretend/fake "medication," a sugar pill. For example, in a placebo-controlled study of one hundred children with ADHD, fifty children will receive the actual medication x and fifty children will receive a placebo. Again, this is under "blinded" conditions: the pills look the same and cannot be identified. When all children have completed the study, the "blind is broken," and the hidden list of what the children were actually receiving is revealed. When the ADHD symptom improvement in each group is compared, the medication group should have improved more than the placebo group. If this is the case, one can conclude that the medication is effective because no doctor or child knew which children were receiving the medication x.

Why would some children get better with a placebo? Wouldn't you expect none to get better? Well, remember that a typical clinical study involves the subject coming in every week to meet with a doctor. In these meetings, although it is not therapy, the doctor does understand the difficulties the child faces, and can communicate his or her support, educate the family, and let everyone feel that they are making efforts to improve the functioning of the child. This could have an impact in improving symptoms, perhaps for a *short* period of time, as during a short-term clinical trial. Thus, an issue such as "Did your child forget anything this week?" (previously a big issue, with much frustration, not quite realizing the child was not doing this "on purpose") becomes "No, things are somewhat better; we are developing a new system to help him remember, and haven't been arguing about it this week." This outcome is the result of the doctor/parent interaction, not the medication.

The next feature, "randomization," relates to how the children are assigned to either the placebo or medication x. It is done randomly, like with the flip of a coin. In this way, no child, parent, or doctor can choose which child gets medication x. All of these features (blinded, placebo controlled, randomized) are important in a scientific study of a new medication. For a drug to be approved by the U.S. FDA as an ADHD treatment, it must show, in double-blind, placebo-controlled, randomized clinical trials, that it is better than a placebo in improving symptoms of ADHD. In addition, it must show that it is safe and well tolerated, having a similar number of side effects as the placebo.

The typical outcomes of clinical trials in pediatric ADHD include both safety and "efficacy" (how well it works) assessments. The measures are taken in office visits, which usually occur on a weekly basis, for six to eight weeks and longer in some other studies. Safety assessments can include measuring heart rate, blood pressure, and weight, and recording if any "side effects" occurred, such as a lower appetite or trouble sleeping since starting the medication. Ratings in clinical studies can include a broader view of functioning, at home, at school, and with peers; however, much of the efficacy assessments are centered upon straightforward ratings of ADHD symptoms by a doctor, parent, teacher, and the child as well.

During ratings, ADHD questions such as "Did your child lose any items this week?" or "Was your child fidgety this week?" are assigned a number code for that week: no symptom (0); mild symptom = more than in other children, but not a problem (1); moderate symptom = a problem, interferes with functioning (2); and severe symptom = a big problem, perhaps prevents functioning, happens in multiple places (3). Taking the question "Was your child fidgety this week?" an answer of "No, not at all" would rate a 0. An answer of "Sometimes we notice, and the teachers notice, but it doesn't seem to cause problems" could rate a 1. An answer of "Yes, the teachers give him a squeezy ball to fiddle with, and it distracts others, and at home he is very often moving around in his seat at dinner or doing homework" could rate a 2. An answer of "Yes, it seems to be constant; he is put in the back of the classroom because he is so disruptive, and still the other kids notice him fiddling, dropping objects," or "At home, he is never still unless he is asleep" could rate a 3.

In the past decade, ADHD drug research studies have become longer in duration, which is important to determine how well and how safe these medications are over time, with studies lasting six months or one year, compared with several weeks as was typical in previous studies. More recent studies also involve larger numbers of children (several hundred) and attempt to be more reflective of the society at large, including children from diverse ethnic and socioeconomic backgrounds. Yet, still, the majority of research studies of ADHD medications conducted to date have involved Caucasian school-age boys treated with short-acting stimulant medications for short periods of time.

FROM DRUG DEVELOPMENT TO TREATMENT

This brief summary of the process of drug development demonstrates the strengths and limitations of the process of bringing ADHD (or any) medications to the market for public use. The strengths of drug development and clinical trials are that medications for childhood conditions are increasingly being studied in great detail, at tremendous expense, prior to giving them to children in the general public.

One of the most recent ADHD medications to go through the process of drug development is a nonstimulant medication called Atomoxetine (Strattera). The company that makes Atomoxetine conducted multiple clinical trials involving over 1,000 children before submitting information to the FDA for approval. As of April 2005, more than 6,000 children, adolescents, and adults have taken the medication in clinical trials for ADHD. That is more than any other drug approved for ADHD in the past. This amount of information allows doctors and families to look very carefully at how the medication works and how safe it is.

The case of Atomoxetine is unusual. Oftentimes a medication comes to market with less information, having been given to a relatively small number of children. Remember that once the drug is approved and can be used by the public, many different kinds of children will use it over time. This exposes one limitation of clinical trials: that only small numbers of healthy children with "just ADHD" will be treated in the typical clinical trial of a new ADHD medication. In the "real world," once the drug is approved, millions of children with ADHD will be prescribed the medication. Of these millions, there will be children with all sorts of other medical and psychiatric problems in addition to ADHD. And, we will not know what to expect when they take the medication. Will the medication be just as safe and effective in these more complicated children as it was in the smaller group with ADHD studied in the clinical trial?

Fortunately, there has been progress in drug development for children because the public and government are realizing the necessity of supporting comprehensive research on medications for children. Not only are the clinical trials becoming more in-depth, with higher standards of safety and efficacy, but also once drugs come to market, surveillance of new medications continues.

THE FDA: SUBMISSION OF A NEW DRUG

Let's say that a company has now completed the phases of developing and studying a new ADHD drug. The sponsor of this new drug now submits a "New Drug Application" to ask the FDA to consider approving the drug to be sold and used in the U.S. This application includes all animal and human safety data, information about how the drug works, and how it is made/produced.

Right away, the FDA can refuse to accept an application that is incomplete, for example, if some required studies are missing. The FDA has a review team, made up of medical doctors, chemists, statisticians, microbiologists, pharmacologists, and other experts, to evaluate whether the studies that the sponsor submitted show that the drug is safe and effective for use. All drugs have side effects. "Safe" according to the FDA means that the benefits of the drug appear to outweigh the risks—that is, the drug does more good than harm.

Each reviewer writes up a report containing conclusions and recommendations about the drug application. These evaluations are reviewed by team leaders and directors. Sometimes, the FDA will ask for an advisory committee, made up of outside experts, to help the agency. But these groups are just advisors, or consultants, and they do not make the final decision; the FDA does.

THE FDA: WATCHDOG

After a drug is approved and marketed, the FDA still keeps watch. The FDA conducts inspections of drug production facilities. The FDA has a system of "postmarketing" programs developed to watch for problems with the new medication that did not appear earlier during the drug approval process. This information may be used to update drug information (labeling of drugs) and, sometimes, to reexamine the decision to approve the drug.

The Adverse Event Reporting System (AERS) is a computerized information database for all approved drugs. The goal of AERS is to improve the public health by storing and analyzing safety data for medications. The reports in

AERS are evaluated by a large staff of scientists in the Center for Drug Evaluation and Research's Office of Drug Safety to monitor drug safety. Another program is the MedWatch program, which is used by health professionals and the public to report serious reactions and problems with drugs. All data on the MedWatch form will be entered into the AERS database.

Now that you are more familiar with the complex issues involved in developing medications for children with ADHD, we can move on to current treatments available. Expect that the government and the scientific community will remain committed to obtaining data on the safety and effectiveness of medications for children, from the beginning of a drug's life, and will continue to improve on making this data available to the public.

5

Treatment of ADHD

OVERVIEW

Screening for ADHD should be part of any child's mental health assessment.
AACAP (2007)

The American Academy of Child and Adolescent Psychiatry (AACAP) and the American Academy of Pediatrics (AAP) are large organizations of professionals dedicated to caring for children and their families. Select members of these organizations, child and adolescent psychiatrists (AACAP) and pediatricians (AAP), regularly produce expert reviews on ADHD. Recommendations begin with a discussion of how to arrive at a correct diagnosis, stressing the importance of educating families and children about ADHD. Specific treatment methods for children with ADHD are recommended and described in great detail.

For the purposes of this book, we will discuss treatment of ADHD according to the guidelines by the AACAP. The first recommendation in the AACAP ADHD guidelines is that, *in any mental health assessment,* doctors should look for ADHD by asking specific questions regarding the child's attention span, activity level, and impulse control. This important statement reflects how common and problematic ADHD is in childhood that doctors must be looking for it, even if ADHD symptoms aren't first brought up by families.

To provide best treatment for ADHD, doctors must meet regularly with families over the child's growing years. This regular communication allows for the assessment of ADHD over time. This is important because the types of ADHD symptoms may change over the course of a child's life. Hyperactivity symptoms may lessen for a given child, whereas disorganization in the face of increased school demands becomes more of a problem. In addition, ADHD symptoms may cause different problems over time. Impulsivity may contribute to use of illegal substances such as alcohol and marijuana. Teens with ADHD may act impulsively more often than their peers, accepting an illegal drug without thinking through the consequences. Some teens with ADHD may use an illegal drug to self-treat or "self-medicate" the feelings of restlessness, impatience, and hyperactivity. In other settings, teens with ADHD may be more distracted and unfocused, such as when learning to drive a car. Doctors and families must be aware of the different challenges facing the growing child and continually reevaluate the presence of ADHD and its impact.

The most successful treatment of a child will follow the most accurate diagnosis, with an understanding of what impacts a child's/adolescent's health at a given time. The most accurate and comprehensive understanding comes from the collaboration of doctor, patient, and family over time. Establishing collaboration is the true beginning to the most successful treatment.

BIO-PSYCHO-SOCIAL APPROACH

The model of psychiatric treatment is an integrated model, combining biological treatment, psychological treatment, and social treatment. For ADHD, biological treatment principally involves medications. Psychological treatment may involve therapy for the child and/or family, addressing self-esteem issues and social and family conflicts. Social treatments can include social support groups for the child, increasing social connections in and out of school, as well as social supports for the family and location of community resources.

PSYCHOPHARMACOLOGY: LOCUS OF CONTROL AND "POWERFUL DRUGS"

Psychopharmacology is the art and science of prescribing medications, "psychotropics," for psychiatric conditions. "The art and science of medicine" is a phrase commonly used to acknowledge that in a way, a doctor is part scientist and part artist. The scientist knows the current medical information on treatments for a condition like ADHD. The artist has skill in listening to, questioning, and connecting with people to describe/paint a picture of ADHD and its treatment with language that is clear to families and children.

Pediatric psychopharmacology involves the prescription of psychiatric medications to children. A pediatric psychopharmacologist is a doctor with particular expertise in the use of psychiatric medications for children. Typically, pediatric psychopharmacologists are child and adolescent psychiatrists who focus their work on learning the art and science of prescribing psychiatric medications for children.

The goal of pediatric psychopharmacology is primarily to assist an individual child to achieve his or her emotional and physical potential. However, the use of medications in children can evoke strong feelings, particularly when it comes to psychotropics. Fears that our society is condoning "medicating" or "drugging" our children are often expressed. As a society, we need to look critically and openly at this issue and understand the role of medications in *any aspect* of our quest for emotional and physical health. As a society we must invest in prevention, education, and social and psychological supports, in addition to investing in the development of medications. This balance must be found in *every field of medicine*, not just in psychiatry.

While society continues to wrestle with this dilemma, doctors must do their best to assist a suffering child and family. Pediatric psychopharmacologists offer medications for the treatment of ADHD based upon recommendations from organizational groups as described above. Medications can offer a child with ADHD more control of his or her body/speech/focus. Medications can be presented to a child and family not as an external force upon a child ("We are *medicating* Joe") but as consistent with an "internal locus of control," an attempt at placing greater control back in the hands of the child. The conversation can be closer to "*You* and your mom and dad are *deciding together* that you will take this medication, because it helps you so much in school and at home."

Children can be quite insightful about how much ADHD medications can help. It is not unusual to hear statements like "I don't need to be silly and hyper and in trouble anymore"; "I got a star for behavior in school, I never got one of those before"; and "I can actually learn something in class, wow!" Children who are openly part of the process of diagnosing ADHD and involved in deciding about the use of medications may be those who continue to seek help over time. At minimum, this process will educate children about themselves and about treatment opportunities. Involvement in this process is critical to foster because when children become young adults, they have to make their own decisions about treatment.

Finally, one additional concern voiced by society, often in the form of media portrayals, is that pediatric psychopharmacology involves the prescription of "powerful" or "potent" medications. "Powerful" in this context suggests that the medication has excess side effects or problems associated with its use as compared with the use of another medication, perhaps a "less powerful" one. All medications have desired benefits ("efficacy") and undesired problems ("side effects," "adverse effects"). ADHD medications, like any medication, have benefits and side effects, all of which should be discussed with families and children.

MEDICATIONS FOR ADHD

Based on many years of scientific study, professional organizations have concluded that medications are the most effective treatment for ADHD. The use of medications for ADHD should involve doctors working together with children and their families, schools, and other mental health professionals such as therapists. In this way, the benefits of medications can be understood by all, and many people can watch for risks of the medications as well. In addition, educational assistance and certain types of therapy can work together, perhaps with an even larger impact than the use of medications alone.

BEGINNING MEDICATION FOR ADHD

When beginning a medication for a child (adolescent), doctors first obtain informed consent from parents/guardians. This involves education about the diagnosis; about the treatments, including medications and nonmedications; about the risks and benefit of using a medication; and about the risks of not treating the problem. This is where the educational process described above becomes specific in communication with a child and family.

MEDICATIONS FOR ADHD: STIMULANT CLASS

Stimulant medications have been shown to be the most effective medication treatment for ADHD. Stimulants are effective in improving ADHD symptoms in the majority of children who take them (approximately 65–75%). This is compared with a much lower (approximately 5–30%) "placebo response." Consider a study that involved 200 children, 100 of whom were assigned (by random, like rolling a dice) to the drug and 100 of whom took the placebo (a sugar pill, an inactive substance). Of the one hundred children taking the drug, about sixty-five to seventy-five of them had improved ADHD symptoms (more focused, calmer, functioning better at school, at home) during the study. Of the one hundred children taking the placebo, perhaps up to about thirty of them had improved ADHD symptoms during the study.

BRAIN OVERVIEW

Before talking about how medications for the treatment of ADHD work, we will have a brief overview of the brain and how brain areas work. The following illustrations are from teaching kits at the National Institute on Drug Abuse (NIDA; http://www.drugabuse.gov/scienceofaddiction/addiction.html and http://www.nida.nih.gov/pubs/teaching/default.html).

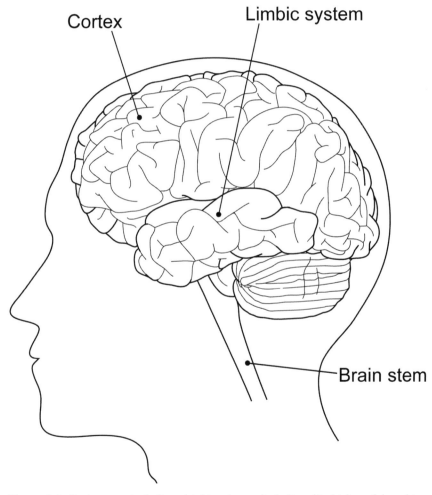

Figure 5.1. Brain areas including thinking (cortex), feeling (limbic), and breathing (brain stem). *Illustrated by Jeff Dixon.*

Age 5 ───► Age 20

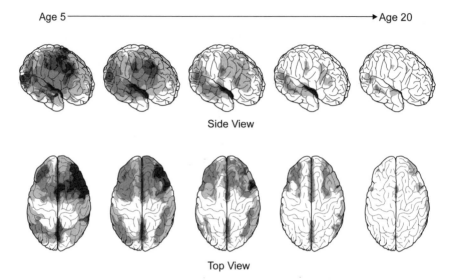

Side View

Top View

Figure 5.2. Maturing brain areas during childhood (shaded areas = maturing areas). *Illustrated by Jeff Dixon.*

The brain is a very complicated organ, composed of many specific areas with specific functions. The main part of the brain, the cortex, is divided into areas that reflect our senses: sight, touch, sound, and taste. The front part of the cortex is the thinking center of the brain. This area helps us to think, manage problems, and make decisions for our daily lives. This part of the brain is important in understanding ADHD, although it is not the only area of the brain important in thinking, planning, and behavioral control. The brain stem is in charge of basic life functions, like your heart beating, your lungs breathing, and allowing you to sleep and rest. The limbic system is in charge of emotions, pleasure, and feelings that motivate us to do important basic tasks like eating, but may also be turned on by illegal drugs in "the pleasure center."

During childhood and adolescence, the brain is growing and developing, along with the rest of the maturing body. Areas that are important in understanding ADHD include parts of the cortex—the prefrontal cortex (shaded area, top view)—one part of the brain that helps us to make good decisions and keeps our bodies and thinking under our control. As can be seen, this part of the brain is still maturing during childhood and adolescence (see page 90–91 for study details).

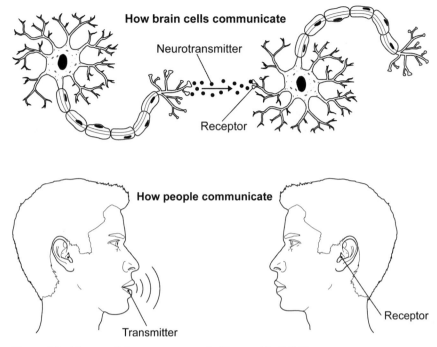

Figure 5.3. Nerve cell "communication." *Illustrated by Jeff Dixon.*

All of these brain areas are made up of nerve cells, called neurons, which communicate with one another as seemingly endless interconnected lines or brain pathways.

The detailed parts of a neuron or nerve cell can be seen below: dendrites, soma, and axons. Chemical information comes into the dendrites and soma from the axons of other nearby nerve cells. The chemical message becomes an electrical message, travelling to the soma, which then produces an impulse ("action potential") that is passed down through the axon to another nerve cell at the terminal.

The action of the nerve cell is at the synapse (space between nerve cells) where the chemical message is released, communicating from one cell to another—the chemical neurotransmission. The nerve cell contains packets of chemical neurotransmitters, such as dopamine (see below). These packets move toward the synapse and are released. Moving across the synapse, the dopamine can attach itself to a specific receptor on a nearby neuron. Once

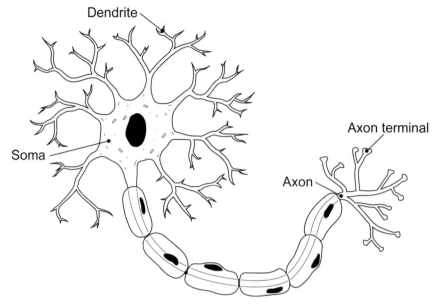

Figure 5.4. Nerve cell structure. *Illustrated by Jeff Dixon.*

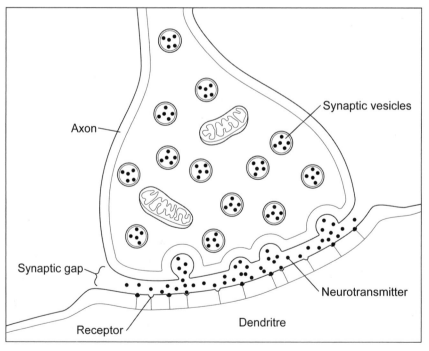

Figure 5.5. Nerve cell synapse. *Illustrated by Jeff Dixon.*

attached to a receptor, a message can be passed, stimulating other actions within the nerve cell, which might lead to turning the nerve cell function on or off.

Importantly, after the chemical message is sent into the synapse, toward the nearby cell, the message is pulled back, or transported back, into the original cell, vacuumed up to be used again later. The brain therefore communicates, neuron to neuron, through chemical neurotransmitters (messengers) to receptors (receivers of information). For a specific area of the brain to work, this message must be passed.

STIMULANT MEDICATIONS: HOW DO THEY WORK?

Stimulant medications come in two main types, methylphenidate (MPH) or amphetamine (typically, mixed amphetamines, or MAS). These medications are mostly swallowed, as pills or capsules, although as we will talk about later, some new forms of stimulants are applied as a patch or a liquid. The medication is absorbed into the bloodstream, then travels to the brain, and it is there that it works to improve ADHD symptoms. Principally, stimulants appear to work by increasing the neurotransmitter (dopamine, norepinephrine) message from one neuron to another.

If the brain cells in the attention area(s) of the brain are not getting enough message between cells, the brain doesn't function well, and does not direct the person's attention to a task at hand. Stimulant medications may have an important effect on motivation areas of the brain in persons with ADHD as well, increasing the "saliency" of the task. It may be that these medications increase the brain's ability to attend to a task, in part by increasing the saliency of a task or increasing the sense of interest or pleasure in performing the task.

The stimulant medications have two ways of increasing the passage of the neurotransmitter message. One method is to *block* the transport of the chemical signal back into a brain nerve cell. As mentioned above, after the chemical message (dopamine) is sent into the synapse, toward the nearby cell, the message is pulled back or transported back into the original cell (vacuumed up, to be used again later). It may be that in ADHD persons, nerve cells are not sending enough messages between cells. Therefore, by blocking the transport back into the cell, more dopamine is now available in between cells, in the synapse. Messages between nerve cells can happen more normally, and the areas of the brain responsible for paying attention, avoiding distractions, and remembering events can function. In addition to this dopamine transporter blockade (DAT blockade), which increases the amount of message available, some stimulants can push more chemical out of the nerve cell. Therefore, in two ways, stimulants can increase the available message between nerve cells in specific parts of the brain.

Therefore, as you can now understand, stimulant medications are not considered cures of ADHD. Instead, simply speaking, they help to provide enough message to pass between nerve cells during the time the medication is in the brain. The medications enter the bloodstream, gradually travel to the brain, have their impact on messages between cells, and then slowly fade away. The medications fade away from the brain as they slowly leave the body, like in the urine, and the ADHD treatment effect is gone.

STIMULANTS: WHAT TYPES ARE THERE?

The original stimulant forms were "short acting": they were swallowed, entered into the bloodstream, and traveled to the brain, with effects lasting roughly three to six hours. Over time, new forms of these stimulants have been developed by drug (pharmaceutical) companies, studied, and approved by the FDA for the treatment of ADHD. The new forms of stimulants mostly involve extended duration forms, which allow children to take a stimulant medication that lasts longer than three to six hours. These newer long-lasting stimulants last either through the school day (6–8 hours; intermediate-acting stimulants) or throughout the school day and into the evening (10–12 hours; long-acting stimulants).

ADHD medications have different ways of releasing stimulant within the body over the day. For example, some are capsules containing a mixture of short-acting medication beads and coated medication beads. As the coated beads travel into the digestive tract, the coating slowly dissolves, eventually leaving only the short-acting medication to be absorbed into the blood system. So, if half the capsule has short-acting beads, half of the total amount of the medication enters the bloodstream right away, and when it starts to wear off, the other half of the capsule, the coated beads, start to enter the bloodstream, to then work for another three to six hours.

In children with mostly school day problems with ADHD, stimulants lasting from six to eight hours may be enough. A child could take a short-acting stimulant in the morning and then repeat that same short-acting stimulant at about noontime, taking it at the school nurse's station with permission from the doctor, nurse/school, and parents. Or, a child could instead take an intermediate-acting stimulant once at home in the morning, and the medication will work through the school day.

There are other children who have serious problems with ADHD symptoms throughout the day and into the evening, children who are so hyperactive all day that they can be dangerous (dash out of the house, jump off furniture, and impulsively push a younger sibling, all in a reckless manner). Or older children and adolescents may be unable to focus and organize themselves to complete evening routines or accomplish homework. These children may benefit from the newer ten- to twelve-hour long-acting formulations. Some of the newer forms of stimulant medications will be discussed in a later chapter.

There is not a specific amount (dose) of stimulant that is best for all children; it must be decided for each individual child. However, there is a typical dose range considered effective and well tolerated, and this is based on research studies of children with ADHD. Higher doses of stimulants generally may be more effective. In addition, a doctor cannot tell which exact stimulant will be best for an individual child. Some children may respond best to one type of stimulant, a methylphenidate type, whereas others may respond best to an amphetamine type of stimulant.

MEDICATIONS FOR ADHD: NONSTIMULANTS

Atomoxetine, a "selective noradrenergic reuptake inhibitor," is an ADHD medication recently approved (in 2003) by the FDA. Atomoxetine is the first medication approved for the treatment of ADHD that is not a stimulant. The drug works by blocking neurotransmitter "reuptake," as we discussed above in talking about stimulants. By blocking the vacuuming up of the chemical signal, norepinephrine, there is more available to pass the message to the nearby nerve cell.

Atomoxetine is a landmark medication, the first psychiatric medication approved for use in children before adults (and the first ADHD medication approved for adults). In addition, it had more research conducted before being released to the market than any prior ADHD medication. Different from stimulants in many ways, this medication can be taken once a day or twice a day, morning or evening time. For some children it may be helpful for sleep and might not reduce appetite as much as the stimulants. Studies have begun to examine whether Atomoxetine may improve other symptoms as well, such as anxiety, depression, or drug/alcohol addictions. Medications may allow a chemical message to be increased in different areas of the brain to allow for different effects; in one area of the brain, there may be more focus, whereas in another area of the brain, the effect might be less worry or depression.

MONITORING MEDICATIONS FOR ADHD

In monitoring ADHD medication treatment, doctors and families examine and discuss both the benefits as well as the side effects they see during the time the child is taking the medication. All medications have benefits, and all medications have side effects. If the benefits are greater than the side effects, the decision is typically to continue the medication, with regular appointments to reassess. If, however, the side effects are serious or they are more noticeable than the benefits, the medication is stopped.

There are no regular blood tests required to monitor ADHD medications. Vital signs and growth parameters should be routinely monitored (see safety section below).

TOLERABILITY/SAFETY OF ADHD MEDICATIONS

In general, ADHD medications are safe and well tolerated when taken as directed over short-term use. As discussed earlier, there is a progression of research in ADHD involving longer treatment periods of study.

The typical, mild physical side effects of stimulant medications include trouble falling asleep (insomnia), stomach upset and abdominal pain, and low appetite, which can be accompanied by weight loss and headache. These side effects are usually mild and sometimes happen with increases in doses of the medication. If these side effects continue and are causing problems, such as the child is tired the next day because it takes him or her more than an hour to fall asleep, then the medication can be stopped and an alternate one considered. Sometimes these side effects only last briefly, such as in the first week of taking the medication, and then appear to lessen or disappear. The side effects should not be judged based on the child taking it once or twice.

Other side effects of stimulants can include mood changes, such as irritability, increased anxiety, feeling more fragile/teary, or becoming more aggressive or having dulled, "blah" emotions. An important message to families and children is that any such persistent change in "personality" (moods) does not need to be accepted, and again, the medication can be stopped and an alternate one considered.

Other side effects of stimulants include the possible worsening of tics (brief unintentional muscle movements, like eye blinking). Overall, ADHD medications do not appear to cause these tics. Tics are common, appearing in early childhood in many children, including children without ADHD or who do not take ADHD medications. However, in some cases medications may worsen tics for a period of time. If the tics are mild and don't bother the child, and the ADHD medication is helping very much, children can continue the treatment, and the doctor and parents can observe the tics over a longer period of time. Tics tend to fade over time on their own.

Side effects of Atomoxetine include upset stomach and fatigue or tiredness. Atomoxetine may not cause insomnia like the stimulants and may not reduce appetite as much; however, as with stimulants, some children may become more moody on these medications. Thoughts of harming oneself, like suicidal ideas, can happen during a medication treatment, including ADHD treatments. There is no evidence, however, that any ADHD medication *causes* suicidal thoughts or actions. It may be that certain children are more vulnerable to them, perhaps those children with a mood disorder (depression) in addition to ADHD. It may be that in those children, if they do not tolerate the medication well; feeling more edgy, restless, or moody; or have trouble sleeping, then they may be more likely to think of harming themselves.

Scientific challenge: Other long-term concerns include the effects of ADHD medications on growth or on brain development. This is an important area to investigate but a complex one. Consider how one would determine whether any medication has an impact on growth or brain development. A study of this would need a huge number (hundreds of thousands, millions) of children, including children with the condition (ADHD) who are on and off medication over many years and also including children without the condition who are also followed over many years, from childhood to young adulthood. Then one would need a very good test that could identify development or lack thereof and that would be relatively easily measured (height, for example). To test for brain development, costly state-of-the-art brain-imaging technology would be needed.

Despite the challenges, researchers are looking at the effects of stimulants on growth and brain development. It appears that the majority of influence on a child's height is genetics/family height and not the influence of a stimulant medication. There is no current evidence that stimulants cause brain damage.

A recent ten-year brain-imaging study by scientists of the National Institute of Mental Health (NIMH) found that multiple brain areas in children and adolescents with ADHD were 3% to 4% smaller than those of children who don't have the disorder. Brain volume was abnormally small in the group of ADHD children who had never been on medications. As mentioned earlier in this chapter, it may be that the brains of children with ADHD are slower to mature and develop and that medications do not cause this delay.

ADHD medications including stimulants and Atomoxetine can increase heart rate and blood pressure mildly. There is no current evidence of serious

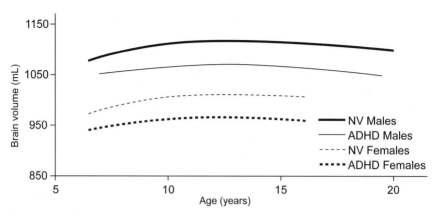

Figure 5.6. Brain development (brain volumes) in ADHD children and children without ADHD (normal volunteers; NV) over development. http://www.nimh.nih.gov/science-news/2002/brain-shrinkage-in-adhd-not-caused-by-medications.shtml. *Illustrated by Jeff Dixon.*

heart damage or medical risk beyond these effects. This is a particularly important area to study. Again, you need to compare the presence of heart problems in huge numbers of children who do not have ADHD with their presence in children who have ADHD and children who have ADHD and are treated with medications. There is current controversy about how best to identify heart problems in children with ADHD before and during medication treatment. Current recommendations stress the importance of asking about a child's previous heart problems or symptoms of possible heart problems, such as racing heart rate or passing out ("syncope") without explanation. Also heart problems that may run in families should be asked about, such as having a relative who was born with an abnormal heart. The evidence suggests that these medications are safe for healthy children, but it may be that children with certain medical conditions, like heart problems, are at risk for serious adverse effects.

OTHER (NONAPPROVED) MEDICATIONS FOR ADHD

In addition to the stimulant medications and Atomoxetine, doctors will prescribe medications that have not been approved by the U.S. FDA for the treatment of ADHD in children. This means that they have not been studied and presented to the FDA in the necessary manner to receive the FDA's stamp of approval. As we discussed, once medications are approved by the

FDA for any condition, they are available for doctors to prescribe for other age groups (children) or other conditions beside the ones they were approved for. This is called "off-label use."

COMBINED PSYCHOPHARMACOLOGY

In those children with more than one psychiatric disorder, such as ADHD plus depression, anxiety, or drug use, the doctor must decide which problem should be the first one to target with medications, if medications are indicated. The doctor tries to best understand which problem is more severe on a daily basis. For example, a child may have a lifelong history of ADHD and then develop a major depressive disorder episode in the teen years. The focus of treatment then shifts from one area (ADHD) to another (depression).

Treatment is for the whole child by understanding all of his/her problems. But, when disorders are significant enough to warrant medication, the medication must be *targeted* at specific issues. In this way, one can determine whether the medication is helping or not. For example, if the decision is that the child with ADHD now has serious depression with low interest, sleep, and energy and with hopelessness, then an antidepressant should be targeted at those symptoms, and the doctor will judge the child's response based on improved interest, sleep, and energy. Once these depression symptoms are improved, then the symptoms of ADHD can be reevaluated and targeted.

THERAPIES AND INTERVENTIONS

Among the behavioral therapies, behavioral parent training (BPT) and classroom interventions are well-established treatments for ADHD, having been around for decades. Behavioral training may be most effective for certain children with ADHD (and their families). Complex behavioral plans may be more difficult for lower-income families, families with a single parent, or parents with a low education. For these interventions and therapies to be effective, one must develop a detailed plan and stick with it, very consistently, over time. Practical matters in certain homes and schools may interfere with this.

Overall, behavioral training has not been shown to be more effective than medications in specifically improving ADHD symptoms, and it is not known if these short-term interventions will have a lasting impact on a child's behavior. Behavioral training in many ways is more complex to study and to use than a medication. We need to support investigations about using behavioral techniques for children with ADHD and their families and support the cost of studying and providing services that are effective.

As with medications, professional organizations review the evidence backing these treatments to let the public, doctors, and therapists know which are the most effective. For example, the American Psychological Association (APA) has a specific group of professionals dedicated to assessing these treatments. The APA considers BPT and behavioral school interventions to be well-established, scientifically supported treatments.

The Multimodal Treatment Study of Children with ADHD (MTA Study)

The Multimodal Treatment Study of Children with ADHD (MTA Study), sponsored by the NIMH, compared medications, behavioral treatment (including intensive BPT), a combination of both, and community care.

The study included over 500 children with ADHD aged seven to ten years and involved several medical centers in the U.S. and Canada. Four interventions were compared: 1) behavioral intervention alone, including a) intensive parent training and education, b) classroom behavioral management training for teachers, c) social skills training, d) computer assisted instruction, and e) a summer treatment program; 2) state-of-the-art medication management; 3) a combination of medication and behavioral intervention; and 4) routine community care, in which the doctors and families decide what to do on their own (e.g., prescribe medications, give advice, etc.).

Children in all four treatment groups improved in their ADHD symptoms over time. The most effective treatment groups were interventions 2 and 3; each of these groups used medication. The combination treatment (3) was most effective in improving troubled family relationships, social skills problems, oppositional behavior, and poor school performance. Combined treatment was better than medication alone for those children with additional psychiatric problems, like anxiety disorders.

Behavioral Parent Training

BPT uses consequences, reward systems, and discipline. Parents learn how to identify a child's behavior that they want to increase (positive behavior) or want to decrease (unwanted behavior). They then learn how to reward good or positive behavior by using praise, positive attention, and rewards. Unwanted behavior is reduced by ignoring it and by using a "time-out" technique and other forms of discipline. Punishment should be very consistent and should immediately follow the behavior.

Scientific studies in children with ADHD have shown this type of behavioral training to reduce parents' stress levels, increase the parents' knowledge and skills about how to handle children with ADHD, lead to improved interactions between children and their parents. Overall, younger children with ADHD are more appropriate subjects for behavioral training compared with adolescents. Other issues, such as whether parents are not emotionally well themselves or have little support from other family members, may impact whether the behavioral training works. Parents and children need to be committed to change and work hard at improving behavior and relationships.

On a side note, these programs do not include physical punishment. Children should never be struck in any way. Hitting, spanking, or any physical punishment is no longer acceptable. Children need to learn that we do not communicate with each other through physical means, and that we use our words. We do not threaten, intimidate, or physically hurt each other. This is no way to change a child's behavior for the best. Hitting teaches one way of interacting with the world and increases the chance that the child then becomes physical with others to try to change their behaviors, such as in schools or when he/she becomes a parent.

Classroom Behavior Interventions

Behavioral interventions have been used in the classroom for decades for children diagnosed with ADHD. Teachers use behavioral classroom interventions to help ADHD children follow classroom rules and get along with classmates.

Techniques are similar to BPT, with use of verbal praise, effective commands, rewards, or time-outs. Behavior modification systems for the classroom must also be clear and consistent to help change and improve behaviors. Some simple examples include a daily report card. The report card has several behavioral goals: improved academic work and behavior, and improved relationships with other children. The teacher records the child's success with the report card. The child can earn a reward (a special meal, time alone with the parent) when he/she meets the goals (not shouting out in class, not getting out of him/her seat). Scientific studies have examined these interventions in children with ADHD and found them to be effective in improving behavior in the classroom.

Academic (Schoolwork) Interventions

Academic interventions try to increase a child's school performance, not just his/her behavior. Children with ADHD often have other academic problems, like learning problems, which are specific problems with math, reading, or writing. These interventions may include pairing the child with ADHD with another child who does not have ADHD and who is doing well in academics. Other more recent attempts include having the children with ADHD study with a computer program. A computer program can provide school material in a new, interesting way, with the child given the chance to interact with the work perhaps more so than in a regular classroom. Other attempts include trying to shorten the task requested such as a fifteen- to twenty-minute quiz as compared with a sixty-minute quiz. Children with ADHD can keep their focus during short chunks of time, so splitting up the schoolwork into smaller pieces can help.

Compared with the other interventions (parent and behavioral classroom), academic interventions have not been shown in studies (yet) to have the same positive effective for children with ADHD. There is not yet the same amount of study and proof for these interventions. However, researchers will continue to investigate these interventions for children with ADHD.

Social Interventions

Children with ADHD who improve in their social problems can function better over time. Social interventions can include attempts to improve social skills (listening, responding) and problem solving in relationships with others (sharing, turn taking). During these therapies, children with ADHD can improve their abilities to make and keep friendships. These interventions are commonly called "social skills groups" or, in schools, "lunch bunches." These groups can be formed at clinics, at schools, or in camps.

Combined Interventions

The combination of medications and behavioral therapies may be the most effective treatment for children and families with ADHD. Adding in behavioral therapies and parent education and training may provide a large impact on a child's health and the health of the family; however, this impact may not be specific to ADHD symptom improvement. At this time, there is no convincing evidence that a combination of treatment is much better than medications alone *for ADHD symptoms*. As mentioned above, the MTA study showed a very similar effect for combined interventions and stimulant treatment alone.

Future studies can continue to examine which behavioral interventions are effective for which children with ADHD (and for which families) and what the impact of these treatments is in combination with medications. It may be that behavioral programs show continued impact on a child's behavior over time, which is different than medications, which appear to work only during the time the medication is in the child's system.

Alternative Treatments for ADHD

There is no current scientific evidence to support the use of alternative treatments for ADHD, like electroencephalographic (EEG) biofeedback or "neurofeedback" or "neurotherapy." Attempts to compare these methods with placebo have not shown a clear benefit.

6

Complications and Associations with ADHD

U
nderstanding the approach to treatment for a child with ADHD is an important first step in treating the whole child. As with other medical conditions, ADHD does not always occur in isolation. Although sometimes ADHD appears to be the primary issue causing problems in a child's life early on, this can change over time. Children can also be quite resilient and can recover from illness, such that a child with several problems in early years can end up with ADHD alone as he/she enters adulthood. The emphasis underlying this chapter is the need for collaboration, a relationship with the child and family, and an open mind to be watchful for additional problems/disorders during a child's development. Then, we must approach the assessment and management of these issues with the same diligence as we have done with ADHD.

A psychiatric or medical disorder, including ADHD, does not always occur alone. Other problems can emerge over time. It is very difficult to conclude, however, that the first disorder (ADHD) caused the other problems or disorders. As briefly mentioned in Chapter 2, other psychiatric conditions ("comorbidities") often are found in children with ADHD. Sometimes it seems that these other conditions are caused by the symptoms of ADHD. But, of course, we cannot be sure of this. Therefore, we can speak about complications of

ADHD that *may seem* directly related to the disorder (driving accidents caused by ADHD inattention) and associations with ADHD that *do not appear* to be caused by the disorder (depression, learning disabilities), although they are commonly found in persons with the disorder.

During a clinical evaluation, doctors ask about a wide range of possible psychiatric problems, in addition to ADHD, including depression, anxiety, and substance use, to name a common few. If there is more than one identified problem (ADHD plus depression), it is important to determine which is "primary," the most impairing, most frequent, and/or most bothersome/severe problem. This is a critical point in understanding how one approaches treating children with psychiatric complexities.

The primary disorder, from a psychiatric perspective, becomes the first target of medications. With success in treating this primary problem, then the other problem(s) are reexamined to see whether treatment of the primary problem has lessened these other issues. If so, it may appear then that the primary problem "caused" the other symptoms. However, if the treatment of the primary problem doesn't change the other symptoms, then it appears more likely that these problems are independent, separate issues.

For example, if symptoms of depression or anxiety are present but are milder on a day-to-day basis as compared with ADHD symptoms and dysfunction, then treatment should begin with ADHD. Similarly, if illegal drug use is intermittent, and relatively milder in its impact, treatment can and still should begin with ADHD. After successful ADHD treatment, depressive and anxiety symptoms and drug use can be reexamined.

SADNESS, DEMORALIZATION, AND MAJOR DEPRESSIVE DISORDER

Children with ADHD can become quite discouraged by academic and relational struggles. Efforts to pay attention, organize, and focus on details can be stressful and time and energy consuming. The child can feel demoralized, be confused as to why he/she cannot accomplish academics to his/her expectation, have negative views of self, and develop a sense that he/she is incapable, not intelligent, careless, and the like. In addition, anger and frustration from parents/teachers can be heaped upon the child as some of the misperceptions about ADHD previously discussed are enacted: "If he wasn't lazy, he would do better;" "If she cared, she would study;" "He can do it when he wants to."

In some (perhaps the more vulnerable) children, a chronic stressor such as undiagnosed ADHD could increase the risk of a major depressive disorder (MDD) episode. In others, it may be that MDD was likely to happen given any stressor, not just ADHD. Symptoms such as sadness or reduced interest, with reduced (or excess) sleep, low (or excess) energy, low appetite, and excessive guilt for a period of 2 weeks or longer, may be consistent with an MDD episode. In major depression, sadness is pervasive and may be accompanied by hopelessness and thoughts of suicide. MDD may be more likely to occur in children with a family history of MDD. MDD is a serious psychiatric illness that needs to be treated as an individual problem, with consideration of therapy, antidepressant medication, and social supports. If present in a child with ADHD, MDD becomes the primary disorder, with treatment focused on resolving the depression before any other treatment is considered, such as for ADHD.

In other children with ADHD, sadness can be milder, coming and going according to the academic difficulties caused by ADHD. In this case, other areas of the child's life are pleasurable, the child remains interested and active in life outside of school, and there is not the full set of symptoms consistent with MDD as described above. Treatment then proceeds with ADHD as the primary disorder, with the expectation that an effective ADHD treatment will yield an improvement in mood, confidence, and esteem.

IRRITABILITY AND THE SPECIAL CASE
OF PEDIATRIC BIPOLAR DISORDER

The majority of children with ADHD can be frustrated. Demands placed upon them may be more than they can handle. Children then respond with frustration at moments, such as when faced with a long, complex school assignment or when asked to do a multistep task that requires more organizational skills than they possess. These moments can be expected, certainly in young children, given their relatively underdeveloped coping abilities. Frustration can appear as moments of "irritability," with yelling, an impulsive toss of an object, a or minor push of a sibling.

Irritability with a capital "I" is different. Children with consistent, intense, severe levels of anger and irritability represent a smaller group within all children with ADHD. These children can have prolonged outbursts in which they are threatening, assaultive, or destructive. Outbursts can continue for many minutes and can recur multiple times in a given day or week. The child can make specific threats that can be particularly violent and destructive. In addition, there can be periods of sadness, hopeless, and despair, and even thoughts of wanting to be dead or statements that the child should never have been born in the first place. There can also be periods of "euphoria," or unusual levels of silly, goofy, giddy moods that are inappropriate for the situation.

This degree of very unusual mood swings from sadness to severe anger to unusual silliness is *not* consistent with most of the children with ADHD. It is consistent with a mood disorder, such as bipolar disorder in adults. In adult bipolar disorder, there are periods of sadness as well as euphoria or irritability. The symptoms of adult bipolar disorder include *distinct periods* of one or more weeks of these mood symptoms (plus other symptoms as noted below). However, children's moods seem to occur differently, more often appearing abnormally disturbed on a more regular basis. Children can "cycle" into violent anger, unusual silliness, and extreme sadness all within a day, as compared with distinct periods of days to weeks in adults.

In part, this is where the current controversy of bipolar disorder in children lies, in that mood symptoms in children and adults appear to occur in different patterns. In addition, some scientists believe that because adults with bipolar disorder can have elevated moods or euphoria, to be diagnosed with childhood bipolar disorder, children must have euphoria and not just extreme irritability.

Despite this difference of opinion, experts in this area would agree that to make the diagnosis of bipolar disorder, there must be a combination of mood problems *and* other symptoms: sleep disruption (such as sleeping less by 1–2 or more hours, yet the child still has excess energy); fast, "pressured" speech (very difficult to interrupt); excess energy; sexual focus or acting out; and grand plans that are unusual for their age (starting a business, driving a car, running the home as if the child were truly the adult in charge). At times, there can be "psychotic" symptoms, symptoms out of touch with reality, such as hearing voices when others are not there ("hallucinations") or suspicion of others' intentions, such as people are trying to harm the child or poison the child when this is not true ("paranoia"). This collection of symptoms occurs on a regular basis, accompanying the severe mood disturbance. Again, to stress the point, these are not children with an occasional tantrum. This is chronic, very unusual, disturbed behavior and emotions.

The scientific thought process in regard to childhood bipolar disorder can be dramatically simplified by these points: 1) children are brought to psychiatrists by their concerned parents because of severe mood problems, oftentimes that place the child and others at risk of injury, even death, or cause serious disruption in school or in social or home life; 2) these mood symptoms are *not* similar to those of most children with ADHD and are *not* similar to those of children who are depressed or oppositional; 3) these mood symptoms are not caused by clear medical problems; 4) these mood symptoms appear even when there are no clear environmental stressors (like abuse); 5) these symptoms appear most similar to adult symptoms of bipolar disorder; 6) adults with bipolar disorder often recall the beginnings of mood problems in early childhood/

teenage years; 7) adults whose bipolar disorder appears particularly severe or chronic seem to have more symptoms of persistent and frequent anger, not just high, euphoric moods; and 8) children diagnosed with bipolar disorder demonstrate an improvement in their mood symptoms after "mood stabilizer"–type medications approved for adults (and now recently approved for children).

In looking at this thought process, we can understand the scientific efforts ongoing across the country to try to best define this group of children. The goal is to understand these severely ill children, to the best of our current abilities, and study them in tremendous detail, including describing their symptoms, levels of intelligence, educational abilities, "comorbid" conditions, medical conditions, environmental stressors, genes, and brains through imaging tests. By describing these children, and by treating and following them over time into their teens and adult years, we can better answer the important questions "Will my child always have these mood problems?" and "Will he/she need medications or treatment all his/her life?" and "Is this going to be just like adult bipolar disorder when he/she grows up?" We do not have the answers to these critical questions yet. It is likely that, in the past, children with bipolar disorder were diagnosed as having other conditions such as "severe ADHD," "severe oppositional or conduct disorder," or "agitated depression."

Part of the concern with the study and treatment of bipolar disorder in children is the use of mood-stabilizing medications or antipsychotic medications, medications whose side effects over time may be more serious than others. Although these concerns are valid, uncertainty should not prevent the study, treatment, and understanding of these disturbed children. Finally, the study of these children can and should, in part, occur in the context of ADHD. It is easy to imagine that the combination of marked restlessness, impulsivity, and short attention span combined with mood instability, rage, and hopelessness is a particularly serious and potentially lethal combination of problems.

WORRY AND SELF-DOUBT

Anxiety can affect children with ADHD struggles as well. Children with ADHD can become anxious, worried about school failure and about not living up to expectations. At times, children can spend many hours in efforts to compensate, and they can organize and organize and organize but not get much done. For example, a child might color code a notebook, copy over notes, and arrange and rearrange piles of schoolwork or books on shelves, but not produce any actual work. Or, a child can sit in class, anxiously hoping not to be called on, aware of his/her lack of preparedness for class, and feeling panicky, and eventually avoid school altogether.

There are children whose anxiety is the primary disorder. In these children the anxiety symptoms come first in a given day, or a given moment. The anxiety is all-consuming. These children may have a clinical anxiety disorder, such as panic disorder, generalized anxiety disorder, or obsessive-compulsive disorder.

Major depression and anxiety disorders need a treatment that is focused on these serious symptoms and should take priority in the general treatment plan of a child with ADHD. Although ADHD symptoms are serious, impairing, and chronic, major depression carries the risk of suicide, and clinical depression and anxiety disorders can interfere with day-to-day existence in ways greater on an acute (short-term) basis than ADHD. In addition, the treatments for ADHD (such as stimulants) can at times worsen/exacerbate feelings of anxiety and sadness, which is not desired in a child already suffering. Once he/she is stable, with only minimal or mild symptoms of anxiety or depression, a child's ADHD can be reassessed and an ADHD-specific treatment plan, including medication, can be initiated or reinitiated. Oftentimes, the recommendation is that some period of stable mood occurs before beginning or resuming ADHD treatment.

SUBSTANCE MISUSE, ABUSE, AND DEPENDENCE

Children with ADHD appear more likely to abuse illegal drugs, including alcohol, than children who do not have ADHD. Importantly, adolescents with ADHD may begin abusing substances earlier than adolescents without ADHD. It is critical to reduce rates of substance abuse in the early teen years because this may be the time when addictions occur and they are then very difficult to stop with the entering of adulthood. Because it can be so difficult for people to stop abusing drugs or smoking cigarettes, the goal is to prevent this use in the first place. Once someone is using, it's a much harder problem to solve.

There are several possibilities to explain why there is more illegal drug use in ADHD children/teens than in children/teens without ADHD. First, impulsivity alone may drive the increased substance abuse. A child with ADHD can be extremely impulsive, not thinking before acting, and therefore he/she accepts whatever is being handed to him/her and swallows or smokes it. When offered some pill/drug/drink/smoke, one would hope that a child would say, "What's that pill?" "Where did you get it?" and "What's in it?" and "What does it do to you?" These would be natural, thoughtful questions from a child without ADHD, a child with the ability to think before acting. A child with ADHD, however, may just say "OK, sure," with little to no thought. That is impulsivity. Later, when the child is facing a parent, he/she may be quite able to state all the risks of drugs, understand why he/she shouldn't take drugs, and have genuine remorse that he/she acted so impulsively. However, that does not mean that he/she wouldn't act impulsively again.

Now, of course, we know all children/adolescents can be impulsive, and can take drugs or drink alcohol at any given moment. Yet, the important difference, as with all ADHD symptoms, is that impulsiveness for an ADHD child is often how he/she interacts with the world. These are not just rare moments of poor childhood judgment. These children (who have the hyperactivity-impulsivity type of ADHD) are repeatedly acting in an impulsive manner.

The second reason why children with ADHD may use more drugs or alcohol than children without ADHD is that illegal drug use in children with ADHD may be a form of "self-medication." Self-medication means that a person is using a substance, often a drug of abuse or alcohol, to feel something good or not feel something, such as sadness or anxiety. They are using an illegal drug as if it were an approved, legal medication, for a specific purpose. When you ask a person who has a substance abuse problem if he/she recalls when the problem began, very often it is clear that the substance use started after another problem, such as sadness, anxiety, or academic struggles.

One specific drug, nicotine in tobacco, is particularly interesting as a form of self-medication. Smoking cigarettes may actually cause an increase in dopamine, the chemical that is therapeutically increased by stimulant medications (see Chapter 5). By increasing dopamine, the child/teen actually may be slightly more focused at times. Others report feeling more relaxed, calmer, and less "hyper" or restless with smoking. So cigarette smoking may be a child/ teen's attempt to treat his/her inattention or hyperactivity-impulsivity. However, of course, we would never suggest that a child with ADHD smoke to improve his/her ADHD symptoms given the physical hazards of cigarette use, including lung cancer. As will be discussed in a later chapter, research on new medications in ADHD is examining the role of nicotine-type medications (using the chemical action of nicotine without the toxins in cigarettes) in treating ADHD.

We will combine the factors given above to provide a short case example. Jack is a fifteen-year-old boy who has come in for treatment with his parents because of their concern with his smoking of cigarettes and marijuana and because they caught him with alcohol in his room. He is nearly failing ninth grade and "doesn't care"; he does not associate with his close friends anymore and spends much of his time in his room or smoking cigarettes on the back porch. His parents are smokers but do not approve of this for their son and are concerned he will not pass ninth grade. In meeting with Jack, we learn he is a bright boy, who made A/B grades until seventh grade, when he felt he couldn't keep up with the schoolwork and felt he couldn't manage switching classes or remembering all his different teachers' requests. Jack remembers the first day he smoked cigarettes "at the corner" around back of the high school. It was after failing a history examination. He had forgotten to study for the test and had made multiple careless mistakes while taking it. He has felt increasingly down about himself and smokes to "feel better, happier, or just not as stressed or something ... it just helps." In talking with Jack and his parents, we learn that he had been diagnosed with ADHD as a young child but was never treated.

As this case shows, oftentimes there is a family history of similar problems (drug or alcohol use/abuse), which likely are influential in the child's problems. Studies have found that children with ADHD have more relatives with substance use disorders. Children with ADHD and a substance use disorder may be more likely to be from a home with a first-degree relative (parent, sibling) who has a substance use disorder. The risks associated with substance use disorders may be different depending on the substance being used, such as alcohol or illegal drugs.

It is quite complex to try to determine which "risk factor" is most responsible for a problem, or which problem running in a family "caused" this problem in the child. Is it the ADHD in the parent that caused the child to have ADHD, which then increased the child's chances of abusing drugs, or is it the drug addiction in the parent that increased the risk for the child to have a drug problem? Or, maybe the trouble is the environment around the child—seeing a parent using drugs or alcohol—and not just the genes inherited from that parent?

The one very good piece of news on the topic of substance abuse and ADHD is that scientists have shown that if children with ADHD are treated with medications for ADHD effectively, these children do not have an increased chance of abusing drugs. These data lie in sharp contrast with fears that ADHD medications will *increase* the rates of drug abuse. Why ADHD treatment appears to reduce rates of illegal drug use may be explained by any number of reasons. The ADHD treatment may drive down levels of impulsivity, enabling the child to think for longer periods of time, weighing the risks of taking a drug before doing it. The ADHD treatment may also effectively replace the self-medication role of illegal drugs, enabling the child to focus, be calmer, and stop looking for alternate (illegal) drugs to treat the symptoms. Maybe the treatment of the child with ADHD has some impact on the parents, who realize that they need to quit using drugs themselves, and thus better themselves, and that is then seen by the child, who is inspired not to use drugs anymore.

However, even if, in general, ADHD treatment does not worsen drug use, there should be some degree of concern by the general public about the potential abuse of ADHD medications, whether by children with ADHD or otherwise. Monitoring of medication use in ADHD patients is recommended, and doctors should keep track of the number of pills they prescribe per month and speak with the family/child if it seems that he/she is running out of medication sooner than expected.

To clarify terms for a moment, "drug misuse" refers to the improper use of a prescription medication, such as a college student taking twice the dose of stimulant to stay up all night to do a paper. "Abuse" is when the pattern of misuse has accompanying problems. "Drug dependence" typically implies serious, frequent, impairing substance use, including physical withdrawal when discontinued.

Teens with ADHD can misuse, sell, and abuse medications, and improper use of prescription stimulants is a known, increasing problem on college campuses in particular. ADHD medications are known as "study drugs." Some students believe that stimulants help them with concentration, studying, and alertness. A portion of these students likely have undiagnosed ADHD and are self-medicating with someone else's medication. Others may have a primary substance use problem. Some may have both ADHD and a substance problem, along with depression, anxiety, and other psychiatric conditions that commonly occur alongside drug misuse/abuse.

In thinking about the risk for abuse of ADHD medications, it is important to recognize that they work in different ways in the body as compared with illegal drugs, which are supremely addictive. With these illegal drugs, there is a high likelihood of continued drug abuse or dependence (e.g., with cocaine). Brain studies help us understand how illegal drugs, like cocaine, can be so addictive. Cocaine enters the bloodstream and very rapidly enters the brain to exert its effect on "reward centers," and then it is very quickly gone. This pattern gives a high rush, then a quick withdrawal, leading to a desire to regain that high. This leads to using again. And then again. And then again.

In comparison with this rapid brain entry of a highly addictive drug like cocaine, ADHD medications enter the bloodstream and the brain much more slowly. ADHD medications then leave the brain and bloodstream gradually. This is not the "profile" of a drug of abuse. There is not the same likelihood of getting a quick high and wanting more. However, you could imagine that the risk of abuse is likely different among ADHD medications. Although not the same as a highly addictive drug like cocaine, the short-acting, quick-release forms of stimulant medications are more easily abused than the once-a-day, long-acting forms of stimulants. The short-acting medications enter the bloodstream relatively quickly, then decline, whereas the once-a-day extended release forms of stimulants enter the bloodstream more gradually over the course of hours.

SOCIAL IMPAIRMENTS AND DEFIANCE

Social and relational conflicts for persons with ADHD have been alluded to throughout this book. It is understood that ADHD symptoms can interfere with making and maintaining friendships for children. For children, impulsivity, difficulty waiting in line, or waiting to speak can cause great conflicts in class, at recess, and in other settings. It is very common to hear about children who are not asked to birthday parties, to family gatherings, onto sports teams, to gymnastics classes, and the like, all because of their "immaturity" (code word for hyperactivity-impulsivity).

Trouble with social relationships could be considered one of the most significant problems that can accompany ADHD. Other children and adults can see the ADHD children as being impolite and intentionally trying to be irritating or frustrating. Studies have shown that children with ADHD are ranked lower on a list of preferred children, have fewer close friendships, and are rejected more than others.

These social and relational problems can have a negative impact throughout one's life. As children with ADHD age into teen and young adult years, the inattention, not listening, and forgetting symptoms may become more problematic in relationships that become increasingly complex. In more mature relationships, one expects to be listened to, that requests are remembered, that possessions are not lost, and that forms/taxes/household bills are managed in an organized fashion. Studies of adults with ADHD have shown increased rates of family conflict, including divorce. Consider the tragedy if symptoms of ADHD, misunderstood over years, cause so much conflict between two adults that they separate and divorce. This has tremendous impact on the adults and can lead to financial strain and great emotional pain. In addition, the children of this marriage undoubtedly suffer.

Although not part of the typical ADHD symptoms, some rating scales or questionnaires include questions about self-esteem, confidence in self, moodiness, and interpersonal conflict. Not all children or adults will have low self-esteem, although many children describe themselves as limited in some fashion, or as "stupid" or "bad" at times, such as when struggling with friendship conflicts, getting in trouble at school, and receiving low grades.

Although many children with ADHD may feel bad about their social problems, others mainly interact socially with a defiant stance. "Oppositionality" or oppositional defiant disorder (ODD) includes a recurring pattern of negative, defiant, disobedient, and hostile behavior toward adults/authority figures. ODD may be the most common co-occurring "comorbid" condition in children with ADHD.

Children with severe ADHD may be seen as oppositional in much of their interactions because they do not listen to most requests/directions and act impulsively and intrusively in most interactions. In addition to not sustaining focus on what is expected of them, children can struggle with pulling their focus from what does hold their attention—videos, television—with great conflicts resulting over disengaging with such activities. However, for some of these children, the parents will admit that the child does want to get along, follows rules, and usually apologizes for not doing what is requested of him/her when the parents finally get his/her attention. For others, there is a consistent defiance of authority figures that clearly goes beyond the symptoms of ADHD.

When present, ODD symptoms often appear to improve and respond to ADHD treatment; studies often show a reduction in symptoms of ODD as ADHD symptoms improve. For example, as a child with ADHD settles down, and is able to sit still, listen, follow directions, and sustain his/her focus in the classroom, you can imagine that this child becomes less disruptive, less argumentative, more respectful, and less defiant.

Maybe this means that ODD symptoms are just an expression or sign of severe ADHD. Then one could conclude that ODD is not really a separate problem. However, the presence of ODD in childhood may increase the risk of later "conduct" problems: major violations of societal norms or criminality. For others, the presence of ODD in childhood may increase the risk of mood problems over time. In these children, the negativity of ODD may indicate that there is an underlying depression or bipolar disorder that will surface late in childhood or into adulthood. We do know that ODD occurs commonly in children with ADHD. Unfortunately, at this time, we do not know what to expect of ODD symptoms over time.

In trying to understand more about ODD, scientists study the family and the environment of children with ODD. The homes (and the parents) of children with ODD have been found to be more negatively oriented. Parents may be less consistent with setting rules or limits in the home and less consistent with how they talk to their children. This type of home environment may influence the development of symptoms of ODD in children.

EDUCATION

In terms of the academic and educational outcomes of ADHD, scientists have asked several important questions: 1) what are the academic characteristics of children with ADHD? 2) do the academic and educational problems last a long time? 3) does ADHD treatment improve academic performance? and 4) how can we improve academics and education in children with ADHD?

Overall, the conclusions are not surprising. Children with ADHD have lower academic performance and more educational problems. They are more likely to be expelled, be suspended, or repeat a grade compared with children without ADHD. These problems appear to persist and not just happen over one year. Individual children can improve in their grades because of being more on task, less careless, and able to complete work. However, it is not easy to demonstrate improved grades in ADHD studies; it is far easier to show improvement of ADHD symptoms, as was discussed in an earlier chapter.

Future studies will continue to investigate the impact of ADHD treatments on reading, writing, and mathematics skills, as well as on the ability to keep children in school, not suspended or expelled. As was discussed previously, social problems in children with ADHD can have a huge impact on later life, as, obviously, academic failure can too.

One area of increasing concern is the impact of ADHD on college success. The good news is that more and more adolescents with significant psychiatric problems are functioning at a higher level and are able to go to college. With greater knowledge about psychiatric problems in childhood and advances in treatment, adolescents can achieve at or near their best ability. But, some of these teens remain vulnerable and struggle when they become independent.

You can imagine a high school senior with ADHD who gets support from parents and friends, receives treatment, and sticks with a consistent routine, doing quite well academically. Then this young adult heads to college. In college, he is responsible for figuring out where classes are, how to get his clothes clean, where to get money, and how to find a quiet study space. This situation becomes overwhelming, and he puts off studying, is less organized, and quickly starts to fail in his classes.

Given this possibility, it is important to stress the necessity of planning and finding local support (therapist, organizational counselor, psychiatrist) for all youth with ADHD heading off to be independent, whether to college or to live and work on their own. Otherwise, it can be too quick and abrupt a transition from "adolescence" to "young adulthood."

MEDICAL COMPLICATIONS AND SAFETY

Children with ADHD have higher health care use and costs than children without ADHD. Children with ADHD can have more frequent use of the emergency room because of accidents, which follow high levels of impulsivity. Children with ADHD can be admitted to the hospital more often than children without ADHD, including with longer hospital stays and more frequently with significant head injury or other serious health events. Families can spend more time at the pediatrician's office in efforts to find an effective treatment for ADHD.

Given this, it is vital to emphasize prevention and safety with children with ADHD. Children with ADHD must be made to wear bike helmets, and basic street safety and public safety must be emphasized. Supervision must be strict because clinically significant impulsivity can be lethal. Not only can children with ADHD be reckless in play, but they can also be unsafe in other public places, dashing across parking lots, leaping off walls, or climbing precariously into trees.

In addition, as children enter adolescence, they can have earlier sexual activity, more frequent changing of sexual partners, and less use of birth control methods. All of these behaviors can increase the risk of sexually transmitted diseases. Teen pregnancies can also occur more often in girls with ADHD, and boys with ADHD can become fathers at a greater rate than those without ADHD. Needless to say, if a teen with ADHD becomes pregnant, she faces the possibility of early labor or complications in the pregnancy because of her age. The baby, the next generation, then has several risk factors for ADHD: genetics (mom with ADHD) and environment (pregnancy complications, possible low income, stressors). This cycle can be avoided with straightforward conversations with the adolescent about safe sexual practices and the impact of a pregnancy on his/her life.

DRIVING DANGERS

One of the most recent concerns of the broader impact of ADHD in adolescence is related to motor vehicle safety. Studies of teens with ADHD have been developed to try to examine the way they drive and whether impulsivity or inattention/distraction can increase the risk of accident. This information can be gathered by asking teens to report past driving accidents and compare that record with that of teens without ADHD. In addition, specialized "driving simulators" have been developed to study teens as they drive. These simulators are akin to video games, which include an actual life-size car, with a screen in front that plays a video of the road ahead. Different challenges arise, creating a simulation of driving down the street, with stop lights, animals darting into the road, children crossing crosswalks, and other cars entering and exiting traffic lanes.

Based on self-reported histories, young adults with ADHD have more speeding or traffic citations than their non-ADHD peers. They can have their licenses taken away or be involved in multiple car accidents. They can have less general knowledge about cars and rules of driving, and demonstrate worse decision making when driving. Interestingly, some studies have recently been done that actually look at the impact of medication on driving performance. Specifically, medications may result in fewer instances of speeding, less erratic speeding, teens taking more time turning the car, and less inappropriate braking.

Direct conversations about car safety must start early in the adolescent's driving career. And parents and teens must understand that driving is a responsibility and a privilege, not a right. Any concerns that the teen is not ready to drive or has driven irresponsibly must be taken very seriously. Drinking and driving, having too many friends in the car, speeding, not wearing a seatbelt, and driving and using a cell phone or e-mail all are potential grounds for removal of driving privileges. For some very impulsive or inattentive teens, it may be wise not to even begin driving lessons until later in adolescence or young adulthood. There need not be a rush to "grow up" in certain areas if the responsibility (getting a license) is greater than the youth can handle. In some ways, giving a car to a teen with significant impulsivity or inattention may be a setup for trouble. You may be increasing the chance of a serious, even fatal, accident.

FINANCIAL LOSSES

The personal financial costs of ADHD are most felt in adults with the disorder. This will be discussed in a later chapter. It suffices to say for now that adults with ADHD can have lower incomes and more frequent job changes, and, as a total group of individuals, account for yearly loss in the U.S. of billions of dollars. Given all the complications and associated problems with ADHD, this is not difficult to believe.

SUMMARY

We have considered a very broad range of life problems that can accompany a diagnosis of ADHD in childhood and into adulthood. ADHD has been described as one of the most impactful of psychiatric disorders, with the potential to influence any major life area imaginable. Social and relational dysfunctioning, mood and substance use disorders, academic and educational deficits, health and safety concerns, pregnancy, and financial and occupational impact all have been described in the individual with ADHD. But this is not to suggest that every one of these issues plagues every child with ADHD. There certainly are children with "milder" ADHD and children who have ADHD alone without other prominent co-occurring problems.

This is all emphasized to demonstrate how far our thinking has progressed in the field of children's mental health. We are now studying the child with ADHD in a very comprehensive fashion. We are illuminating the potential far-reaching implications of the disorder. This is not simply about making children "behave" in school. The ramifications of an ADHD diagnosis extend far beyond the classroom.

Our hope is that shedding light on the child with ADHD and the associated problems and complications will advance the level of knowledge in the community and thus enhance preventive efforts and increase the chance that every single child with ADHD will receive comprehensive assessments and the best of available treatments. Now, we will return to the impact of ADHD, although in a more personal setting: the family.

7

How ADHD Affects the Family

F amilies can be thought of as a team of people, working together. To best function, all members of the team must cooperate, and work together, to achieve common goals. For a family with school-aged children, the goal is to get through the work/school week and enjoy the weekends/vacation time together. If one member of the family is consuming more time or energy, that can change the family balance. All members of the family can suffer. When functioning at its best, the family supports growth and happiness in each of the members individually and as a unit.

The presence of a child, or for that matter a parent, with ADHD can upset the healthy balance of a family. The now well-familiar ADHD symptoms can clearly complicate daily living and functioning. Although treatment can have a significant impact on symptoms and improve functioning, education about the disorder may be the first real step in changing the way the family interacts and functions. To understand that the child's (or parent's) ADHD symptoms are indicative of a medical problem and not intentional can provide some relief all around, reducing the mounting conflict/frustration.

Studies have examined relationships between children and parents, including some of the largest treatment studies conducted to date, such as the previously described Multimodal Treatment Study of Children with ADHD.

In studies, children with ADHD have been shown to view their parents (both mothers and fathers) as more demanding and more power hungry than do children without ADHD. Consistent with this, parents of ADHD children can think of themselves as more power assertive or less warm. These conflicted feelings appear to be more likely in those children and parents who have some degree of sadness or depression symptoms.

When looking at parenting and assessing parental stress and low esteem in ADHD families, one should look for levels of depression in the parent(s). In other areas of psychiatry, such as in the treatment of childhood depression, parental depression has been shown to have a significant impact on the child's response to treatment. In other words, children whose parents remain depressed are less likely to fully respond to treatment. Why is this? It's difficult to say; however, as we discussed before, genetics and environment come together in powerful ways to influence the expression of psychiatric illness in children.

In addition to how parents and children feel and act around each other, families report that there is simply less leisure time in households with children with ADHD. Perhaps this is because of the difficulty in negotiating basic routines, leaving little to no time for leisure moments, "family time," or relaxation. Life can become about managing the child, and something can be lost in the process. Because of this, some studies look at how quickly medications become effective in the morning or how long they last in the evening. Also, great effort has been made to assist children and families in learning sufficient organizational skills over time to make daily living more manageable.

Let's imagine a "typical" family, with a mother, father, eight-year-old son, and twelve-year-old daughter. The family has yet to begin treatment for the son's ADHD, is uncertain about the use of medications, and sees that he is managing average grades in school. On a typical school morning, Father leaves the home early for work, and the son, "James," is up at about 6 AM, playing loudly in his room with a train set. Mother stops by and asks him to get dressed while heading downstairs with the daughter, who is practicing a report for school that day.

At 6:20 AM, twenty minutes later, Mother realizes James has not been downstairs and finds him in his room, having emptied out his closet looking for a baseball glove. He is not dressed. She reminds him several times (more loudly each time) to get dressed. She pulls out his clothes and places them in his hands, he nods his understanding of the need to get dressed NOW, and then Mom heads to brush her teeth. Five minutes later, Mom comes back to his room and can't find James. James is now downstairs, climbing up in the pantry to pull down cereal. He has only his pajama bottoms on. Mom grabs his clothes and toothbrush and heads downstairs, hearing the crash of cereal boxes and jars to the floor. James apologizes and fidgets while Mom dresses him.

Now Mom gets James to come for breakfast. It's 6:45 AM, and he is kneeling on his chair, picking at a spot of old food on the table. Mom asks him where his book bag is, which she helped him pack the night before, and he says that he doesn't know. He also can't find his field trip form. This is a form Mom gave to him when he sat down at the table just five minutes earlier. In exasperation, Mom heads off to find his bag and his permission slip and then shepherds him out the door, ten minutes later. His sister is teary, nearly late for school and for her project. James didn't eat breakfast because he was watching something out the window.

That night, sister cries that she was late for school and did poorly on her report. Dad and Mom sit down with James to tell him again that for the family to function in the mornings, he must 1) listen, 2) follow directions, 3) stay focused and on task, 4) not lose items, 5) ignore distractions, and 6) be organized. James nods emphatically, promises to be "better," and admits he got in trouble at school for losing his field trip form.

Not all families struggle to this degree, and, as stated, children's overall functioning can improve notably during treatment. The first step of educating children and families about ADHD is a vital one. Then, as families enter treatment, over time, in-depth discussions can occur about how the family unit functions. This will allow for clarity about the particular weaknesses of family members (a parent with marked disorganization, a sibling with a psychiatric illness of his own), as well as unique challenges at certain times of day (morning routines with the mom home alone) or great difficulty in particular settings (family church). Given this information, treaters and families can work together to tailor a treatment program.

One particular area where families commonly struggle is at home, in the evening or during unstructured time, such as weekends or holidays. When asking about home conflicts, it is very informative to ask about the ADHD child's ability to entertain him/herself. Children with ADHD can have a great difficulty in sustaining their focus, independently and quietly, without being plugged into TV or videos or electronics. This can lead to intrusiveness of the child, boisterous evenings, and much conflict. The child can become a wandering child, going from person to person, looking for stimulus, not finding it consistently, and only getting negative feedback: "Go do something yourself, quietly!" If he/she could sustain focus on a quiet task (reading, drawing, playing a game), not only would he/she have some peaceful downtime to him/herself but so also would the others in the family.

Thus, not only should the assessment of ADHD's impact cover the child's social, academic, and emotional life at school and at play, but it must also account for the life of the family. One must assess the degree of symptoms in the home and the potential conflicts the ADHD symptoms may cause.

We will now move on to a look at the future of ADHD. As will be seen, there is remarkable scientific work being done in the field of ADHD, including genetics, brain imaging, and novel treatments. However, is there similar growth in the study of ADHD and the family? Do the advances in the science of ADHD translate into better lives for children and families? This is the intent, the hope, that we can not only conduct remarkable genetic investigations of ADHD individuals and perform state-of-the-art brain imaging to get details on the size and function of the human brain, but, at the same time, also facilitate clear improvement in the lives of our patients. We want families to be unified, not divided, to reach common goals. This is what it comes down to. This is what the science is about. Better lives for children and families. Let's look into the future with that in mind.

8

Clinical and Scientific Research in ADHD

I n this past decade there has been remarkable growth and advances in clinical and scientific research in ADHD. Scientists and clinicians from around the world are dedicating time, effort, and resources to better our understanding of ADHD. Treatment advances include novel medications in different forms. Scientific advances include remarkable imaging pictures of the brains of children and adults with ADHD.

ADVANCES IN MEDICATIONS

Advances in medications for ADHD include advances in extended release forms of standard stimulants, new formulations (delivery mechanisms), and new nonstimulant medications. The goal is to provide multiple options for children and adults so that treatment can be individualized, meaning not just one treatment to fit all persons.

On this point, a conversation with families about specific medications should include the details about how the medication is taken. If there is hesitation or uncertainty about pill swallowing, this should be discussed, allowing a chance for the doctor to give tips or how-to advice. The child should be involved in the process. As mentioned before, there should be a sense of unity in the discussion, with a consensus that the child is not "being medicated."

This is an opportunity for an in-depth discussion about the practical aspects of taking medication. New forms of medications offer the chance to tailor the treatment to the child (or adult).

Some patients (mostly young children) want medications that are easy to take, such as chewable or sprinkle forms of medications. All these options are now available in the stimulant class of medications, including methylphenidate and amphetamine types of stimulants. These options allow parents to give a medication in a form that is accepted by the child. The last thing everyone needs is a daily confrontation about a pill that is large and hard to swallow.

The newest additions to this type of medication include one that can be dissolved in water (an amphetamine) and a patch form (a methylphenidate) of stimulant. Several medications, including once-a-day types, come as capsules, which contain small beads inside; the capsule can be opened and the sprinkle beads poured out, such as into a spoonful of applesauce. A more recent medication can be opened and dissolved in a small amount of water.

The patch stimulant is somewhat like a clear Band-Aid, which is placed on the hip, under the waistline, and left on all day. The patch contains medication in multiple tiny pockets and slowly enters the bloodstream through the skin. This can provide more flexibility as well, allowing a parent to place the patch on at a certain time, any time of day, and remove it later at any time of day. This can be quite helpful at times, such as on weekends. Also if the child sleeps late, typically he/she cannot take a once-a-day form of medication because it will last too late into the nighttime and impact sleep.

Another new addition to this class of medications is an amphetamine medication that is called a "prodrug." Prodrugs are found in other areas of medicine. They are drugs that become "active" once it is in the body. This prodrug is composed of an amino acid connected to a type of amphetamine. The medication becomes active when it broken down by the digestive system. The amphetamine is released into the bloodstream. The interesting possible benefit of such a medication is that it may be much less abused. Remember that stimulants can be taken in ways not prescribed (not by mouth) as persons with drug addictions try to get high. This medication does not appear to release the same amount of medication if taken in any other way besides by mouth, as prescribed.

Additional nonstimulant medications are being studied as well. This group includes a new long-acting form of an older medication that has been used for ADHD for years but not FDA approved. This medication has noradrenergic action and appears to work by improving brain function in the prefrontal cortex. This is the area we discussed previously, an area of the brain that is responsible for "working" memory, behavioral restraint, attention, and cognition control.

OTHER MEDICATIONS

There are multiple other medications in addition to stimulants and the nonstimulant Atomoxetine that are used to treat ADHD or have been studied in ADHD patients. However, these medications are not approved by the FDA for the ADHD indication; these include antidepressants (bupropion, tricyclic antidepressants, and venlafaxine), clonidine, and various novel agents. Investigational medications include those that may work by increasing levels of dopamine (see Chapter 5) in an indirect fashion. The brain's ability to send messages between nerve cells depends on a variety of chemical messengers called neurotransmitters. It may be that taking advantage of these multiple inputs and complex outputs between nerve cells will provide for other targets for new ADHD medications.

Three of the main reasons that new ADHD medications are needed (beyond new forms of stimulants) are as follows: 1) the side effects of the stimulants, such as low appetite, trouble sleeping, and mood effects; 2) the possibility of abusing stimulants like drugs of addiction; and 3) the limited response some people have, perhaps specifically those who have great difficulty with organization or executive dysfunction. Therefore, any child, adolescent, or adult may not fully tolerate or respond to a given current ADHD medication. It is for these individuals that the advances in ADHD medications continue to be necessary.

STATE-OF-THE-ART BRAIN IMAGING

In select centers across the country and at governmental agencies such as the National Institute on Drug Abuse, scientists are studying the brains of persons with ADHD. The efforts are an attempt to examine the structure (size) and function (how it works) of certain brain areas in people with ADHD, brain areas involved in attention, memory, behavioral control, and organizational tasks such as planning. Brain pictures can identify the relative size and thickness of a brain region, which can be compared with persons without ADHD. Brain pictures can also be taken during brain functioning, such as during a cognitive task, to see how active a brain area is as compared with a person without ADHD.

What is quite extraordinary is that a brain image can now involve multiple pictures of a tiny area of the brain of a person with ADHD, which can then be used to create a three-dimensional replication of the brain area. The scientist can then study the replication on a computer screen and look at the area in its entirety.

Brain-imaging tests can also examine brain circuits, the "highways" within the brain. By examining brain pathways, scientists can determine whether they are faulty, such as not allowing normal signals to pass from one brain area to another. It may be that in ADHD, the size and function of specific brain areas are not that different from those of people without ADHD, but the communication, the highways, is disordered. One technique to observe the brain's highways is called diffusion tensor imaging (DTI). DTI is an imaging technique used to detect changes in brain circuitry based on diffusion or movement of water molecules within the brain pathways. Magnetic resonance imaging (MRI) can be used as a measure of white matter structure, allowing investigation of brain changes during normal development or in the case of abnormal development.

Other imaging tests can allow a scientist to observe the activity or functioning of a select brain area while a person is completing a specific task. An active area of the brain "lights up" on imaging scan because of blood flow or energy consumption (basic energy components in blood, glucose). Therefore, to test brain function in ADHD, one could assign a task that demands very close attention to several different details (determining the color and shape on a note card) while the person is lying in a brain imaging scanner. While the task is being done by the person, pictures of specific areas of the brain can be taken.

In some of the most exciting research in ADHD, brain functioning studies have demonstrated that specific brain areas responsible for attention to have abnormal (low) brain activity in persons with ADHD as compared with those areas in persons without ADHD. Studies have also shown some return to "normal" brain activity when ADHD medication is given. Other recent highlights include the examinations of the dopamine receptors in brain regions of ADHD subjects; lower than normal dopamine release is seen in persons with ADHD.

Researchers at the National Institutes of Health's (NIH) National Institute of Mental Health (NIMH) recently published an important, one-of-a-kind study. This group examined the brains of children with ADHD over time. The researchers scanned 446 participants ranging from preschoolers to young adults at least twice over approximately three-year intervals. They chose the age when the brain (cortex) starts to thin after puberty (the brain thins during the teen years as part of a normal brain process to reduce unused brain nerve cell connections).

In this study, the brains of children with ADHD were found to mature in a normal pattern, but the maturation was delayed three years, on average, in some brain regions, compared with youth without the disorder. The delay in ADHD children's brains was most prominent in regions at the front of the brain's cortex, areas important for the ability to control thinking, attention, and planning. Besides these differences, both groups showed similar waves of brain development and maturation.

For example, in both the ADHD and non-ADHD control groups, sensory and motor control brain areas peaked in thickness early in childhood, whereas the frontal cortex areas responsible for higher-order executive control functions peaked later, during the teen years. These frontal areas support the ability to suppress inappropriate behaviors and thoughts, focus attention, and control movement, functions often disturbed in people with ADHD.

However, circuitry in the front and sides of the brain that coordinates information from sensory areas with higher-order functions showed delay in youth with ADHD. One of the last areas to mature, the midpart of the prefrontal cortex, lagged five years in those with the disorder. Conversely, the *motor* cortex matured faster in youth with ADHD, in contrast with the late-maturing *frontal* cortex, the area intended to control it. The researchers suggested that this mismatch might yield the restlessness, fidgety motor symptoms of ADHD.

The head of the NIMH Child Psychiatry research team suggested that the main finding (delayed brain development) may explain why some youth seem to "grow out of" the disorder, why symptoms of ADHD lessen over time. Previous brain and imaging studies did not detect the developmental delay because they focused on the size of the brain's cortex. These differences were found only after a new brain image analysis technique allowed the researchers to pinpoint thousands of cortex sites in hundreds of children and teens, with and without ADHD. The remarkable detail of this study is that among 223 youth with ADHD, half of the 40,000 cortex sites attained peak thickness at an average age of 10.5 years, compared with age 7.5 years in youth without ADHD.

The authors did report, however, that brain imaging is still not ready for use as a diagnostic tool in ADHD. Although the delay in brain development was notable, it was only detected when the researchers examined very large numbers of children. Therefore, it is not yet possible to see this brain delay from a brain scan of just one individual. The diagnosis of ADHD remains a clinical one based on taking history.

DISCOVERING ADHD SYMPTOMS IN ADULTHOOD

Scientific challenge: How do you determine whether ADHD *continues* into adulthood?

Take a group of 100 children with ADHD. Have them come to your office in five, 10, 15, and 20 years, beginning after their first appointment at age six.

Interview them specifically about the presence of each ADHD symptom, and impairment caused by the ADHD symptoms, at each time point in their life: ages 11, 16, 21, and 26.

Now, this is the most important next step: how do you define "continues"? Meaning, if you define *continued ADHD* in adulthood as still meeting *all* criteria of ADHD later in life, you will get one answer. For example, it may be that 25% of the original 100 children still meet *all* the criteria for ADHD at age 26: six or more symptoms of ADHD, occurring in multiple settings, etc.

However, if you define *continued ADHD* in adulthood as still meeting *most* of the criteria of ADHD later in life, the rates may be much higher. For example, this second definition (*most* of the criteria of ADHD) may capture people who had four or five symptoms of ADHD (not six symptoms) at age 26. Or, it may be that most of the criteria include people with symptoms exhibited in just one setting. According to this second definition, 50% of the original 100 children meet this criterion for ADHD at age 26. There are more people that meet these criteria because the threshold is lower: fewer symptoms, present in fewer settings.

Of course, both definitions may be important to study and can provide critical information. One definition tells you that the majority of children will not meet the standard definition of ADHD at age 26, yet the second definition tells us that there is a significantly larger group of children who will still have problems caused by ADHD at this age. The second definition allows these persons to be counted, to be considered as individuals who need assistance, who have impairment.

The explosion of research of adult ADHD includes 1) what the symptoms look like, and how they may differ from symptoms in childhood; 2) the financial and social impact of ADHD in adulthood; 3) the genetics and brain imaging of adults with ADHD; and 4) the response to treatments in adulthood. This explosion of study has occurred in the recent past.

Common ADHD complaints in adulthood are not specifically listed as symptoms in the American Psychiatric Association's diagnostic manual, the *DSM-IV-TR*. However, the symptoms do parallel childhood symptoms. There have been efforts to make the symptom descriptions more adult appropriate.

Self-report ratings/questionnaires have also been developed, which allow adults to see whether they may have ADHD. One tool for adults is the World Health Organization *Adult ADHD Self-Report Scale* (ASRS v1.1), a six-question scale designed to test for adult ADHD. The ASRS instrument is publicly available at http://www.med.nyu.edu/psych/psychiatrist/adhd.html. Tools like these are particularly important, because, despite the evidence of severe problems accompanying ongoing ADHD symptoms into adulthood, few adults at this time are receiving treatment for ADHD. Perhaps with more clear symptoms and education, treatment opportunities will follow.

The limited treatment is caused in part by hesitation by primary care physicians to diagnose and treat adult ADHD. In addition, adult psychiatrists are just beginning to learn about ADHD in adulthood. Remarkably, training in adult psychiatry has not included information about adult ADHD. Instead, the only psychiatrists trained about ADHD are child and adolescent psychiatrists. This is an important area of needed training and education for the future. Child and adolescent psychiatrists are so in demand to provide clinical care and academic research that it is difficult for them to lead the way in adult management and research as well. A collaboration of adult and child psychiatry will be important to continue growth in this area.

The changing course of ADHD symptoms can be observed in both inattentive types of symptoms as well as hyperactivity-impulsivity types of symptoms. For example, in the inattention domain, the childhood symptom of procrastination can be seen as slowness and inefficiency in the adult, and an inability to organize in the child seen as poor time management in the adult. Examples of adult-appropriate questions to determine inattentiveness include the following: Do you make a lot of mistakes at work? Is this because you are careless? Is it hard for you to keep your mind on work? Trouble listening, so evident in the child who needs a repetition of requests, can be different in adults, who can appear to be listening, getting the sense of a conversation, yet miss much of the important details. Yet, with maturity and a sense of social expectations, adults may be more able to hide these symptoms than a child.

The changing course of ADHD symptoms from childhood into adulthood is also evident in the hyperactivity-impulsivity core domain. For example, in this domain, the child who squirms, fidgets, or cannot stay seated may be seen in adulthood as an adult who is not able to sit through meetings as an adult; the child who runs and climbs excessively may be seen as an adult on the move more than others or one who drives too fast. The child who cannot play or work quietly may be the adult who selects a very active job. The child who blurts out answers may become the adult who is constantly trying not to jump in when others are working or talking. At times, when the urge is so great, an adult with ADHD may miss much of conversations because he/she is so focused on not interrupting. Other examples of hyperactive/impulsive symptom questions include the following: Is it hard for you to slow down? Do you feel like you (often) have a lot of energy and that you always have to be moving, always "on the go"? Do you talk a lot? Do people complain about your talking?

Again, as an adult, one has more ability to determine the types of work and leisure time one is involved in. Therefore, adults with ADHD may be more able to choose certain careers or hobbies that work better for their symptoms. Such choices may be sales, active labor (construction), hairstyling, or acting/theatre. Or, adults may expend their excess energy by working two jobs and spending long hours at work.

To make the diagnosis of adult ADHD, the adult must have problems with six or more of nine symptoms of inattention or hyperactivity-impulsivity, persisting for at least six months, with impairment in at least two types of settings, and symptoms dating back to childhood. Self-report of symptoms by adults is a reliable method of diagnosis, but the mental health professional or primary care physician should obtain a full history. Clinicians should ask about family history, academic/work demands, marital functioning, and physical health.

ADHD IN ADULTHOOD

Surveys of adults with ADHD have identified frequent comorbid depression, anxiety, and substance use disorders. Often, ADHD is not diagnosed and is missed as a contributing problem in an adult with a known psychiatric or medical problem. For example, the case of Mr. L (below) will demonstrate that ADHD may be missed in adults who 1) are diagnosed as depressed, perhaps during increased work demands, when it is in fact the ADHD symptoms that are impairing functioning; and/or 2) do not follow medical advice because of procrastination, forgetfulness, and impulsivity.

As with children, problems like mood and anxiety disorders and substance use disorders can be thought of as exacerbated by ADHD or as separate problems. As in children, the treatment of adults with ADHD and other emotional problems will begin with treatment of the disorder that is causing the most day-to-day problems.

Perhaps it is ADHD itself causing the trouble, or perhaps ADHD plus feelings of depression or anxiety. Either way, this results in tremendous social costs in this country. Also, untreated adults can have many problems associated with work. They may change jobs frequently because of restlessness, impatience, or poor work performance and may be fired more frequently.

Because of these work problems, adults with ADHD may have lower incomes than adults without ADHD. Recent estimates of household income loss associated with adult ADHD range from $8,900 to $15,400 per year. For example, take two workers at a local factory, one with ADHD and one without. The worker with ADHD, with poorer performance and consistency in work, is at a lower pay level, which results in $10,000 less money every year as compared with his peer without ADHD. Over ten years of working for that company, his peer has made $100,000 more than he. In taking all adults with ADHD in this country together, recent estimates suggest that the country loses $100 billion a year, making ADHD one of the most costly medical conditions in the U.S.

In addition, adults with ADHD have been shown to have lower education levels than others without ADHD. For example, adults with ADHD may not graduate from high school as much as their peers. If adults with ADHD continue education after high school, they can be less likely than their peers to graduate from college.

MR. L: ADULT ADHD

The following is a brief case example of ADHD in adulthood. It is important to understand that these symptoms can impact an adult's ability to work, function, and be healthy, and all these areas can be inextricably tied together.

Mr. L is a thirty-nine-year-old married man who came to his regular medical physician's office for a routine annual visit four years after his last appointment. In reviewing medical records with the doctor, Mr. L admits that he has come to the office only once in a while over the past eight years, and he has not been following dietary and exercise advice. He remains slightly overweight, is a cigarette smoker, and has a family history of heart disease. Mr. L has had brief episodes of "minor" depression.

Mr. L is an automobile salesman and tells his doctor about his concern regarding longstanding forgetfulness and disorganization, which are increasingly obvious since his recent promotion to a job with a lot of office-based paperwork and administration demands. Mr. L describes a recent educational assessment for his nine-year-old daughter, who may have ADHD; Mr. L was struck by the similarities with his own early childhood academic struggles: "I saw my childhood being repeated in my daughter."

Mr. L completes a self-report symptom checklist and returns with his wife at the next doctor appointment. Mr. L rated all six of the screening questions for ADHD as occurring often or very often, "Essentially all the time, basically every day." The majority of the additional questions are rated with a similar frequency. Mr. L also describes problems at work, at home, and socially. His wife, who manages the household finances, agrees that these symptoms have caused great frustrations and conflicts over the years. She has "always suspected he has ADHD" because she had a friend with ADHD growing up; "Otherwise I may have divorced him years ago . . . thinking that his not listening and forgetfulness were intentional or lazy or insensitive."

Mr. L describes full DSM-IV ADHD symptoms beginning in early elementary school and into high school and college. Although he did maintain average or better grades, he was held back in kindergarten for being "immature," his academic performance was consistently inconsistent, and he "just got by through cramming" during the last year of high school and into college. His primary occupation has been sales, with little demanding administrative work and consistency in routines over the years, with his wife handling the majority of home tasks, billing, and scheduling. However, his mood has suffered in the context of change in demands and routines, such as in his current promotion, leaving him feeling "like I am in grade school again, lost in paperwork." Therefore, he is coming in now to his primary care doctor, asking for help, because he believes he may be fired from his new job once his lack of organization and follow-through is noticed.

This case highlights several areas of clinical note. First of all, we are introduced to Mr. L as a middle-aged man who is not taking care of himself physically. He has several major risk factors for cardiovascular disease: excess weight, smoking, lack of exercise, poor diet, depression, and a family history of heart disease. When we learn about his difficulty with organization and follow-through, it is not difficult to see how ADHD can be directly involved in the development of these factors.

Second, we learn that Mr. L has long been a car salesman but has received a recent promotion. This should be good news, but the administrative demands are taxing his abilities. In addition, we learn that his wife has taken over the home finances, given his deficits, and that their marriage has been held together thanks to his wife's understanding. Had she not been knowledgeable about ADHD, Mr. L could have been reporting a divorce as another stressor and loss in his life. Finally, we learn that these symptoms, or deficits, have been present throughout his life, partially compensated for or hidden thanks to the support of others (his wife) and the consistency of occupational (nonadministrative) demands.

So, moving forward, treatment of Mr. L will include monitoring for symptoms in multiple areas: Is he more consistent in maintaining his own physical health, making appointments, and remembering them? Is he able to sustain his focus more consistently at work, listen to directions, and be organized in his daily work? Is he more attentive in the home, able to remember tasks he promised to do, and able to listen to his wife and family's requests? With education, a medication treatment, and possibly organizational assistance, we can expect Mr. L to have an excellent global response. We can expect to make a tremendous impact on his personal and professional life.

In this chapter, we have discussed the recent and ongoing advances in clinical and scientific research in pediatric and adult ADHD. The medications available to persons with ADHD continue to increasingly offer a wider range of options, making it possible to tailor treatments to an individual patient. Incredible technology available to scientists is providing first-ever looks at the details of the human brain in its developmental course, in persons both with and without ADHD. Brain scans are giving us pictures of brain areas of critical import (areas that allow us to attend to tasks), and the study of the chemical messenger dopamine continues to develop. There is still no brain scan, blood test, or pen-paper test to diagnose ADHD. Perhaps in the future.

9

Conclusions

Are you still paying attention to this book? Good for you and your brain. You now well realize how remarkable the human brain is in its "simple" ability to pay attention. You realize that we should not take for granted this fundamental brain function. Individuals with ADHD struggle with this basic skill, along with the constellation of specific symptoms we have discussed (e.g., distractibility, impulsivity, hyperactivity).

We have discussed an individual's life course of ADHD, as well as the remarkable, still developing scientific exploration of ADHD. This conclusion will review the key points of prior chapters. However, as we have discussed, attention to detail is an important ability, and thus the details of prior chapters should not be overlooked, skimmed, put off ... you get the idea.

Symptoms of ADHD have their origins early in a person's life, are present and unusual in their frequency and in their severity as compared with peers, and typically occur wherever the individual is (e.g., home, school), causing significant problems. The symptoms cannot be explained by another condition, such as a medical condition or psychiatric disorder or learning disability. Although historically ADHD has been considered to be a disorder of childhood, it has become quite clear that many children do not "grow out of it," and ADHD can continue to cause tremendous problems into adulthood.

The diagnosis of ADHD is made through a careful "clinical history." People like to have "objective evidence" (seen by others) of ADHD. However, at present, there is no paper-pencil test, and neither is there a blood test or brain x-ray to diagnose ADHD. This state of the science reflects the fact that we do not know exactly what causes ADHD. It is most likely caused by a combination of the influences of genes and the environment. A child's brain may start out abnormally formed because of the influence of genes and may then be additionally damaged by an environmental insult, such as tobacco smoking by the mother during pregnancy. Overall, the child's brain may be slow to mature, to develop, and may never reach the same size or function as that of a "healthy" child. We do not yet know if the brain may be influenced, in a positive manner, by later attempts at treatment, such as with medications. There is no compelling evidence of a negative impact on brain growth and development because of ADHD medications.

Clinicians highly trained in clinical assessment of child mental health disorders, including ADHD, are child and adolescent psychiatrists. Although pediatricians commonly assess and prescribe medications for children with ADHD in this country, at present, the complexity of the knowledge base, the increasing array of medication options, and the presence of complex psychiatric comorbidities together place too great a burden on primary care pediatricians.

In the careful clinical assessment of the child with ADHD complaints, common areas of psychiatric comorbidity ought to be assessed: mood symptoms (sadness, anger/irritability, euphoria), anxiety symptoms (social fears, anxiety attacks, generalized fears, obsessions, compulsions), disruptive behaviors (defiance, stealing, lying), substance misuse (alcohol, marijuana), and eating disorders (intentional weight loss). During this clinical evaluation, the determination is made whether there are other significant psychiatric problems, or if the associated symptoms are caused by ADHD (child demoralized because of school failure) or are less in their daily impact (mild social anxiety). In addition, clinicians expect to find academic, social, and familial struggles in children with ADHD. Therefore, the effort is to intervene early, before the child is suspended, expelled, or is required to repeat a grade or before health and safety is impacted, such as with an accident because of carelessness or hyperactivity.

Critically, as with any area of medicine, recall that the treatment response to ADHD medications should back up the diagnosis; treatment should yield clear and convincing reduction in ADHD symptoms specifically. Generally speaking, approximately 75% of children with ADHD respond well to medication treatment.

We discussed the treatment of ADHD in some detail, but first started with an overview of the drug development process. Look to the government and the scientific community to remain committed to thoughtful research on the safety and effectiveness of medications for children, from the beginning of a drug's life. The details of this scientific endeavor should be publically available and clinically meaningful, as well as helpful to the individual child, adolescent, or adult with ADHD.

The treatment of ADHD has been described according to the recently updated guidelines by the American Academy of Child and Adolescent Psychiatry (AACAP). Keeping our clinical focus, we must not lose sight of the simple tenet of working with children and families; the most successful treatment of a child follows the most accurate diagnosis, and the best diagnosis is built upon an understanding of what impacts a child's or adolescent's health over time. To obtain accurate and current information, one needs a collaboration among treater, patient, and family. Given that trust, a working relationship between treater and family and patient, the integrated treatment of ADHD can begin.

It is most likely that the optimal treatment for ADHD will combine biological treatment, psychological treatment, and social treatment. For ADHD, biological treatment principally involves medications. Psychological treatment may involve therapy for the child or family, addressing self-esteem issues and social and family conflicts. Social treatments can include social support groups for the child, increasing social connections in and out of school, as well as social supports for the family, with the location of community resources. Although the broad treatment approach can support patients and families, the evidence determines medications to be the primary, most effective treatment.

As we discussed, stimulant medications are the most effective medication treatment for ADHD. Stimulant medications come in a variety of forms, with short-, medium-, and long-acting preparations, and can come as patches, sprinkles, and liquids. Stimulants appear to work by increasing the neurotransmitter message from one neuron to another to increase the effectiveness of that specific brain area. A similar mechanism is found in the nonstimulant medication, whereas novel medications may exert their effect through indirect pathways to this final chemical transmission. In general, ADHD medications are safe and well tolerated, although our ability to study long-term outcomes such as impact on brain development or heart function continues to develop and may offer new, important information in years to come around the topic of the long-term safety of medications.

We ended the book by looking at the future growth of the field, understanding that ADHD symptoms do not magically disappear for many children or adolescents as they enter adulthood. This has been a critical scientific-medical discovery. The whole field of adult ADHD has grown dramatically, with stunning data about the impact of ADHD on an adult's functioning, the disorder impacting essentially every major life area: relationships, health, education, and economics and occupation. The study of adults with ADHD may be easier to conduct, given the challenges of working with young children and the necessary protections that must be in place for the young. Therefore, the study of adults can move the field forward, taking full advantage of the latest in brain-imaging techniques, genetic examinations, and comprehensive clinical and research-based neuropsychiatric assessments.

CLOSING

The hope is that shining a bright spotlight on the child, adolescent, and adult with ADHD will advance the level of knowledge in the community, in turn increasing the chance that assessments and treatments are requested by patients, parents, and family members. The goal is to intervene *before* all the possible negative outcomes (social, emotional, health, economic, educational) lead to tragic realities. You are welcome to join in the vitally important scientific study and provision of clinical care for childhood mental health and cognitive, behavioral disorders. The scientific and clinical challenges await your dedicated attention.

Appendix A

A Look at Attention Deficit Hyperactivity Disorder (ADHD)

National Institutes of Mental Health. *A Look at Attention Deficit Hyperactivity Disorder (ADHD)*, National Institutes of Mental Health, 2004. Available online at http://www.nimh.nih.gov/health/publications/a-look-at-attention-deficit-hyperactivity-disorder/summary.shtml.

DOES THIS SOUND LIKE YOUR CHILD?

Ricky

Ricky sits on his hands to stop them from moving. "It's like I have a motor inside me going 'brrrrrr' all the time and I can't stop it."

ATTENTION DEFICIT HYPERACTIVITY DISORDER

- Is it hard for your child to sit still?
- Does your child act without thinking first?
- Does your child start but not finish things?

If you answered "yes" to these questions, you may want to read this booklet to learn more about Attention Deficit Hyperactivity Disorder—called ADHD for short. ADHD is a real illness that starts in childhood. It can change the way children act, think, and feel.

Some children with ADHD squirm, fidget, or wiggle all the time and act without thinking. Others seem to be in another world, often staring into space or daydreaming. All of these behaviors may be signs of ADHD. This may sound like many children. But when such behaviors make it hard for a child to do well in school or make friends, ADHD may be the cause.

Parents of these children may know there is a problem, but they may not be sure what the problem is or what to do about it. **Reading this booklet will help you learn what you can do to help your child.**

FIVE STEPS TO UNDERSTAND AND GET HELP FOR ADHD

- Look for signs of ADHD.
- Learn that ADHD is an illness that can be treated.
- Ask your child's doctor for help.
- Talk to your child's teachers.
- Work together to help your child.

STEP 1: LOOK FOR SIGNS OF ADHD

Carlos

"When I read the checklist, I couldn't believe it. I was nodding and saying 'si, si' for each thing. I made many check marks. They all described my son, Juan. It made me want to figure out this whole thing so he could finally get better."

ADHD Signs

Put a check mark next to each one that sounds like your child.
My child often…

- is moving something — fingers, hands, arms, feet, or legs.
- walks, runs, or climbs around when others are seated.
- has trouble waiting in line or taking turns.
- doesn't finish things.
- gets bored after just a short while.
- daydreams or seems to be in another world.

- talks when other people are talking.
- gets frustrated with schoolwork or homework.
- acts quickly without thinking first.
- is sidetracked by what is going on around him or her.

Does this sound like your child? If so, talk with your child's doctor. The doctor can tell you whether your child has ADHD. The doctor can also tell you which treatments can help your child. If you visit the doctor, take this checklist with you.

WHAT IS NORMAL?

Noah

"I do OK in gym class. Library time is the worst. All I hear is 'sssshh.' I tell myself 'Don't talk,' but I never stop myself in time."

NORMAL BEHAVIOR

Most children have trouble sitting still. Many kids don't finish their school-work. Few children sit through meals without tapping, kicking, or drumming. So how do you know what is normal and what is ADHD? Only a doctor can tell you for sure. ADHD behavior doesn't happen in only one place, like at school. It may happen every day in the classroom, on the playground, and at home. ADHD can lead to problems with learning, friendships, and family life.

STEP 2: LEARN THAT ADHD IS AN ILLNESS
THAT CAN BE TREATED

Pearl

"I get in trouble all the time," Pearl tells her school counselor. "My teacher doesn't like me. At recess none of the other kids want to play with me. Am I bad?"

ADHD IS AN ILLNESS THAT CAN BE TREATED

ADHD can make children feel bad about themselves. They may see them-selves as failures, when they are not. They need help with this common child-hood illness.

With the right care, children with ADHD are able to pay attention, control their behavior, and slow their fast pace. With the illness under control, children can grow, learn, and develop better than before.

Kanesha

"Tyronnes's teacher gave me a booklet on ADHD to read. It really helped. I used to think I was not a good parent or that he was not a good kid. Now I know it has been ADHD all along. It's an illness—like Ginetta's asthma. No one is to blame. It's a card we've been dealt. That's all. Now that we know what we are dealing with and how to treat it, it's getting better."

WHAT CAUSES ADHD?

The exact cause of ADHD has not yet been found. ADHD seems to run in families. If a parent, uncle, or grandparent has ADHD, other family members may also develop it. Physical differences in parts of the brain may also have something to do with it. There may not be a single cause, but a few things may come together to cause ADHD.

STEP 3: ASK YOUR CHILD'S DOCTOR FOR HELP

Puran

"I called the community mental health center because you don't need insurance to go there. We met with a child psychiatrist. The doctor asked us questions about how my daughter Shahi acts at home and school. The doctor also wanted to know about any bad things that happened in her life, like when her father died. Then we got some forms for Shahi's teachers to fill out. This was how we found out she had ADHD."

ASKING YOUR CHILD'S DOCTOR FOR HELP

If you are worried about your child's behavior, trust your feelings. Ask your child's doctor for help. Many parents start by taking their child to see a family doctor or pediatrician. Some families go on to see doctors who specialize in childhood problems such as ADHD. These doctors are called **"child psychiatrists"** or **"child psychologists."** Tell the doctor about the behavior that worries you. The doctor will tell you if the cause may be ADHD.

The doctor will also want to look for other possible causes of the behavior. Sometimes children who are dealing with divorce, death, or other problems act in ways that look like, but aren't, ADHD. For this reason, your doctor will ask about things that are happening at home. The doctor will also make sure there are no other diseases or disabilities that might be causing your child's behavior.

Medicine and **"behavior therapy"** are the most common treatments for ADHD. Medicine for ADHD can help children pay attention, finish tasks, and think before they act. Behavior therapy involves meeting with the doctor to work on new skills to make it easier to deal with relationships, rules, limits, and choices. Both medicine and behavior therapy are safe and proven to work. These treatments used together give the best results.

STEP 4: TALK TO YOUR CHILD'S TEACHERS

Fernando

"I am eleven years old and I just did my first puzzle. Before, when I wasn't taking medicine, I'd start but never finish them. I'd end up throwing the pieces on the floor. This time I took a short break, but I stuck with it. And I did it! My mom is really proud of me. I'm proud of me too."

TALKING TO YOUR CHILD'S TEACHERS

Your child's school may be able to help in many ways. Talk to your child's teachers about ADHD.

- Ask if your child is having any problems in the classroom or on the playground.
- Tell the teachers that your child has ADHD, a common childhood illness.
- List any medications your child takes and explain any other treatments.
- Find out if your child can get any special services that help with learning.

To make sure your child gets all the help he or she needs, you can also talk to a guidance counselor at the school.

STEP 5: WORK TOGETHER TO HELP YOUR CHILD

Parents, children, teachers, and doctors should work together as members of a team. Together you can set goals for your child and find the right treatment to reach those goals. Some of the goals families can work toward include:

- helping children feel better about themselves,
- helping children do better in school,
- helping children follow classroom and household rules,
- helping children make more friends, and
- reducing the behaviors that cause problems.

Some children with ADHD also get tutoring or counseling at school. Let your doctor knows about any services provided by the school.

Rachel

"In therapy I work on ways to remember things better. One is called **BHB**. It stands for **B**ackpack, **H**omework, **B**ooks. And I say to myself, 'Have you got your BHB on?' My mom says it to me too. It helps me remember my school stuff."

ADHD IN TEENS AND ADULTS

Many people think of ADHD as a childhood illness, but it can continue through the teen years and into adulthood.

The teen years can be especially hard. With ADHD, people act without thinking first. This can make it hard for teens to make careful choices about drugs, drinking, smoking, or sex. In therapy, teens and parents work on rules, limits, and choices to help things go smoother at home and at school.

ADHD also makes it hard to finish what you start. This can be a real problem for adults. Men and women may have trouble keeping up with the things they need to do at home and at work. Adults with ADHD may lose job after job because of their illness.

At any age, treatment can help.

TIPS FOR PARENTS

Try to learn as much as you can about ADHD. As a parent, trust your thoughts and feelings. You know your child better than anyone else. If you don't think your child is getting the services he or she needs, speak up. Tell your child's doctor or school what you think. And don't stop asking questions.

Remember ADHD can be treated. Keep working to help your child get better. To be your child's best helper, take good care of yourself and stay healthy.

FOR MORE INFORMATION

Attention Deficit Hyperactivity Disorder Information and Organizations are available from NLM's MedlinePlus (en Español).

Appendix B

Attention Deficit Hyperactivity Disorder

N ational Institute of Mental Health. *Attention Deficit Hyperactivity Disorder.* Available online at http://www.nimh.nih.gov/health/publications/adhd/summary.shtml.

INTRODUCTION

Attention Deficit Hyperactivity Disorder (ADHD) is a condition that becomes apparent in some children in the preschool and early school years. It is hard for these children to control their behavior and/or pay attention. It is estimated that between 3 and 5 percent of children have ADHD, or approximately 2 million children in the United States. This means that in a classroom of 25 to 30 children, it is likely that at least one will have ADHD.

ADHD was first described by Dr. Heinrich Hoffman in 1845. A physician who wrote books on medicine and psychiatry, Dr. Hoffman was also a poet who became interested in writing for children when he couldn't find suitable materials to read to his 3-year-old son. The result was a book of poems, complete with illustrations, about children and their characteristics. "The Story of Fidgety Philip" was an accurate description of a little boy who had attention deficit hyperactivity disorder. Yet it was not until 1902 that Sir George F. Still published a series of lectures to the Royal College of Physicians in England in which he described a group of impulsive children with significant behavioral problems, caused by a genetic dysfunction and not by poor child rearing—children who today would be easily recognized as having ADHD.[1] Since then, several thousand scientific papers on the disorder have been published, providing information on its nature, course, causes, impairments, and treatments.

A child with ADHD faces a difficult but not insurmountable task ahead. In order to achieve his or her full potential, he or she should receive help, guidance, and understanding from parents, guidance counselors, and the public education system. This document offers information on ADHD and its management, including research on medications and behavioral interventions, as well as helpful resources on educational options.

Because ADHD often continues into adulthood, this document contains a section on the diagnosis and treatment of ADHD in adults.

SYMPTOMS

The principal characteristics of ADHD are **inattention**, **hyperactivity**, and **impulsivity**. These symptoms appear early in a child's life. Because many normal children may have these symptoms, but at a low level, or the symptoms may be caused by another disorder, it is important that the child receive a thorough examination and appropriate diagnosis by a well-qualified professional.

Symptoms of ADHD will appear over the course of many months, often with the symptoms of impulsiveness and hyperactivity preceding those of inattention, which may not emerge for a year or more. Different symptoms may appear in different settings, depending on the demands the situation may pose for the child's self-control. A child who "can't sit still" or is otherwise disruptive will be noticeable in school, but the inattentive daydreamer may be overlooked. The impulsive child who acts before thinking may be considered just a "discipline problem," while the child who is passive or sluggish may be viewed as merely unmotivated. Yet both may have different types of ADHD. All children are sometimes restless, sometimes act without thinking, sometimes daydream the time away. When the child's hyperactivity, distractibility, poor concentration, or impulsivity begin to affect performance in school, social relationships with other children, or behavior at home, ADHD may be suspected. But because the symptoms vary so much across settings, ADHD is not easy to diagnose. This is especially true when inattentiveness is the primary symptom.

According to the most recent version of the *Diagnostic and Statistical Manual of Mental Disorders* (DSM-IV-TR),[2] there are three patterns of behavior that indicate ADHD. People with ADHD may show several signs of being consistently inattentive. They may have a pattern of being hyperactive and impulsive far more than others of their age. Or they may show all three types of behavior. This means that there are three subtypes of ADHD recognized by professionals. These are the **predominantly hyperactive-impulsive type** (that does not show significant inattention); the **predominantly inattentive type** (that does not show significant hyperactive-impulsive behavior) sometimes called ADD—an outdated term for this entire disorder; and the **combined type** (that displays both inattentive and hyperactive-impulsive symptoms).

Hyperactivity-Impulsivity

Hyperactive children always seem to be "on the go" or constantly in motion. They dash around touching or playing with whatever is in sight, or talk incessantly. Sitting still at dinner or during a school lesson or story can be a difficult task. They squirm and fidget in their seats or roam around the room. Or they may wiggle their feet, touch everything, or noisily tap their pencil. Hyperactive teenagers or adults may feel internally restless. They often report needing to stay busy and may try to do several things at once.

Impulsive children seem unable to curb their immediate reactions or think before they act. They will often blurt out inappropriate comments, display their emotions without restraint, and act without regard for the later consequences of their conduct. Their impulsivity may make it hard for them to wait for things they want or to take their turn in games. They may grab a toy from another child or hit when they're upset. Even as teenagers or adults, they may impulsively choose to do things that have an immediate but small payoff rather than engage in activities that may take more effort yet provide much greater but delayed rewards.

Some signs of **hyperactivity-impulsivity** are:

- Feeling restless, often fidgeting with hands or feet, or squirming while seated
- Running, climbing, or leaving a seat in situations where sitting or quiet behavior is expected
- Blurting out answers before hearing the whole question
- Having difficulty waiting in line or taking turns

Inattention

Children who are inattentive have a hard time keeping their minds on any one thing and may get bored with a task after only a few minutes. If they are doing something they really enjoy, they have no trouble paying attention. But focusing deliberate, conscious attention to organizing and completing a task or learning something new is difficult.

Homework is particularly hard for these children. They will forget to write down an assignment, or leave it at school. They will forget to bring a book home, or bring the wrong one. The homework, if finally finished, is full of errors and erasures. Homework is often accompanied by frustration for both parent and child.

The DSM-IV-TR gives these signs of **inattention:**

- Often becoming easily distracted by irrelevant sights and sounds
- Often failing to pay attention to details and making careless mistakes
- Rarely following instructions carefully and completely losing or forgetting things like toys, or pencils, books, and tools needed for a task
- Often skipping from one uncompleted activity to another

Children diagnosed with the Predominantly Inattentive Type of ADHD are seldom impulsive or hyperactive, yet they have significant problems paying attention. They appear to be daydreaming, "spacey," easily confused, slow moving, and lethargic. They may have difficulty processing information as quickly and accurately as other children. When the teacher gives oral or even written instructions, this child has a hard time understanding what he or she is supposed to do and makes frequent mistakes. Yet the child may sit quietly, unobtrusively, and even appear to be working but not fully attending to or understanding the task and the instructions.

These children don't show significant problems with impulsivity and over-activity in the classroom, on the school ground, or at home. They may get along better with other children than the more impulsive and hyperactive types of ADHD, and they may not have the same sorts of social problems so common with the combined type of ADHD. So often their problems with inattention are overlooked. But they need help just as much as children with other types of ADHD, who cause more obvious problems in the classroom.

Is It Really ADHD?

Not everyone who is overly hyperactive, inattentive, or impulsive has ADHD. Since most people sometimes blurt out things they didn't mean to say, or jump from one task to another, or become disorganized and forgetful, how can specialists tell if the problem is ADHD?

Because everyone shows some of these behaviors at times, the diagnosis requires that such behavior be demonstrated to a degree that is inappropriate for the person's age. The diagnostic guidelines also contain specific requirements for determining when the symptoms indicate ADHD. The behaviors must appear early in life, before age 7, and continue for at least 6 months. Above all, the behaviors must create a real handicap in at least two areas of a person's life such as in the schoolroom, on the playground, at home, in the community, or in social settings. So someone who shows some symptoms but whose schoolwork or friendships are not impaired by these behaviors would not be diagnosed with ADHD. Nor would a child who seems overly active on the playground but functions well elsewhere receive an ADHD diagnosis.

To assess whether a child has ADHD, specialists consider several critical questions: Are these behaviors excessive, long term, and pervasive? That is, do they occur more often than in other children the same age? Are they a continuous problem, not just a response to a temporary situation? Do the behaviors occur in several settings or only in one specific place like the playground or in the schoolroom? The person's pattern of behavior is compared against a set of criteria and characteristics of the disorder as listed in the DSM-IV-TR.

DIAGNOSIS

Some parents see signs of inattention, hyperactivity, and impulsivity in their toddler long before the child enters school. The child may lose interest in playing a game or watching a TV show, or may run around completely out of control. But because children mature at different rates and are very different in personality, temperament, and energy levels, it's useful to get an expert's opinion of whether the behavior is appropriate for the child's age. Parents can ask their child's pediatrician, or a child psychologist or psychiatrist, to assess whether their toddler has an attention deficit hyperactivity disorder or is, more likely at this age, just immature or unusually exuberant.

ADHD may be suspected by a parent or caretaker or may go unnoticed until the child runs into problems at school. Given that ADHD tends to affect functioning most strongly in school, sometimes the teacher is the first to recognize that a child is hyperactive or inattentive and may point it out to the parents and/or consult with the school psychologist. Because teachers work with many children, they come to know how "average" children behave in learning situations that require attention and self-control. However, teachers sometimes fail to notice the needs of children who may be more inattentive and passive yet who are quiet and cooperative, such as those with the predominantly inattentive form of ADHD.

PROFESSIONALS WHO MAKE THE DIAGNOSIS

If ADHD is suspected, to whom can the family turn? What kinds of specialists do they need?

Ideally, the diagnosis should be made by a professional in your area with training in ADHD or in the diagnosis of mental disorders. Child psychiatrists and psychologists, developmental/behavioral pediatricians, or behavioral neurologists are those most often trained in differential diagnosis. Clinical social workers may also have such training.

The family can start by talking with the child's pediatrician or their family doctor. Some pediatricians may do the assessment themselves, but often they refer the family to an appropriate mental health specialist they know and trust. In addition, state and local agencies that serve families and children, as well as some of the volunteer organizations listed at the end of this document, can help identify appropriate specialists.

Knowing the differences in qualifications and services can help the family choose someone who can best meet their needs. There are several types of specialists qualified to diagnose and treat ADHD. Child psychiatrists are doctors who specialize in diagnosing and treating childhood mental and behavioral disorders. A psychiatrist can provide therapy and prescribe any needed medications. Child psychologists are also qualified to diagnose and treat ADHD. They can provide therapy for the child and help the family develop ways to deal with the disorder. But psychologists are not medical doctors and must rely on the child's physician to do medical exams and prescribe medication. Neurologists, doctors who work with disorders of the brain and nervous system,

Specialty	Can Diagnose ADHD	Can Prescribe Medication, if Needed	Provides Counseling or Training
Psychiatrists	yes	yes	yes
Psychologists	yes	yes[*]	yes
Pediatricians or Family Physicians	yes	yes	no
Neurologists	yes	yes	no
Clinical Social Workers	yes	no	yes

* As of October 2006, Louisiana and New Mexico laws and regulations allow psychologists who have completed specific training and meet other requirements to prescribe psychotropic medications. The other 48 states and the District of Columbia allow only physicians to prescribe medications.

can also diagnose ADHD and prescribe medicines. But unlike psychiatrists and psychologists, neurologists usually do not provide therapy for the emotional aspects of the disorder.

Within each specialty, individual doctors and mental health professionals differ in their experiences with ADHD. So in selecting a specialist, it's important to find someone with specific training and experience in diagnosing and treating the disorder.

Whatever the specialist's expertise, his or her first task is to gather information that will rule out other possible reasons for the child's behavior. Among possible causes of ADHD-like behavior are the following:

- A sudden change in the child's life—the death of a parent or grandparent; parents' divorce; a parent's job loss
- Undetected seizures, such as in petit mal or temporal lobe seizures
- A middle ear infection that causes intermittent hearing problems
- Medical disorders that may affect brain functioning
- Underachievement caused by learning disability
- Anxiety or depression

Ideally, in ruling out other causes, the specialist checks the child's school and medical records. There may be a school record of hearing or vision problems, since most schools automatically screen for these. The specialist tries to determine whether the home and classroom environments are unusually stressful or chaotic, and how the child's parents and teachers deal with the child.

Next the specialist gathers information on the child's ongoing behavior in order to compare these behaviors to the symptoms and diagnostic criteria listed in the DSM-IV-TR. This also involves talking with the child and, if possible, observing the child in class and other settings.

The child's teachers, past and present, are asked to rate their observations of the child's behavior on standardized evaluation forms, known as behavior rating scales, to compare the child's behavior to that of other children the same age. While rating scales might seem overly subjective, teachers often get to know so many children that their judgment of how a child compares to others is usually a reliable and valid measure.

The specialist interviews the child's teachers and parents, and may contact other people who know the child well, such as coaches or baby-sitters. Parents are asked to describe their child's behavior in a variety of situations. They may also fill out a rating scale to indicate how severe and frequent the behaviors seem to be.

In most cases, the child will be evaluated for social adjustment and mental health. Tests of intelligence and learning achievement may be given to see if the child has a learning disability and whether the disability is in one or more subjects.

In looking at the results of these various sources of information, the specialist pays special attention to the child's behavior during situations that are the most demanding of self-control, as well as noisy or unstructured situations such as parties, or during tasks that require sustained attention, like reading, working math problems, or playing a board game. Behavior during free play or while getting individual attention is given less importance in the evaluation. In such situations, most children with ADHD are able to control their behavior and perform better than in more restrictive situations.

The specialist then pieces together a profile of the child's behavior. Which ADHD-like behaviors listed in the most recent DSM does the child show? How often? In what situations? How long has the child been doing them? How old was the child when the problem started? Are the behavior problems relatively chronic or enduring or are they periodic in nature? Are the behaviors seriously interfering with the child's friendships, school activities, home life, or participation in community activities? Does the child have any other related problems? The answers to these questions help identify whether the child's hyperactivity, impulsivity, and inattention are significant and long-standing. If so, the child may be diagnosed with ADHD.

A correct diagnosis often resolves confusion about the reasons for the child's problems that lets parents and child move forward in their lives with more accurate information on what is wrong and what can be done to help. Once the disorder is diagnosed, the child and family can begin to receive whatever combination of educational, medical, and emotional help they need. This may include providing recommendations to school staff, seeking out a more appropriate classroom setting, selecting the right medication, and helping parents to manage their child's behavior.

WHAT CAUSES ADHD?

One of the first questions a parent will have is "Why? What went wrong?" or "Did I do something to cause this?" There is little compelling evidence at this time that ADHD can arise purely from social factors or child-rearing methods. Most substantiated causes appear to fall in the realm of neurobiology and genetics. This is not to say that environmental factors may not influence the severity of the disorder, and especially the degree of impairment and suffering the child may experience, but that such factors do not seem to give rise to the condition by themselves.

The parents' focus should be on looking forward and finding the best possible way to help their child. Scientists are studying causes in an effort to identify better ways to treat, and perhaps someday to prevent, ADHD. They are finding more and more evidence that ADHD does not stem from the home environment, but from biological causes. Knowing this can remove a huge burden of guilt from parents who might blame themselves for their child's behavior.

Over the last few decades, scientists have come up with possible theories about what causes ADHD. Some of these theories have led to dead ends, some to exciting new avenues of investigation.

Environmental Agents

Studies have shown a possible correlation between the use of cigarettes and alcohol during pregnancy and risk for ADHD in the offspring of that pregnancy. As a precaution, it is best during pregnancy to refrain from both cigarette and alcohol use.

Another environmental agent that may be associated with a higher risk of ADHD is high levels of lead in the bodies of young preschool children. Since lead is no longer allowed in paint and is usually found only in older buildings, exposure to toxic levels is not as prevalent as it once was. Children who live in old buildings in which lead still exists in the plumbing or in lead paint that has been painted over may be at risk.

Brain Injury

One early theory was that attention disorders were caused by brain injury. Some children who have suffered accidents leading to brain injury may show some signs of behavior similar to that of ADHD, but only a small percentage of children with ADHD have been found to have suffered a traumatic brain injury.

Food Additives and Sugar

It has been suggested that attention disorders are caused by refined sugar or food additives, or that symptoms of ADHD are exacerbated by sugar or food additives. In 1982, the National Institutes of Health held a scientific consensus conference to discuss this issue. It was found that diet restrictions helped about 5 percent of children with ADHD, mostly young children who had food allergies.[3] A more recent study on the effect of sugar on children, using sugar one day and a sugar substitute on alternate days, without parents, staff, or children knowing which substance was being used, showed no significant effects of the sugar on behavior or learning.[4]

In another study, children whose mothers felt they were sugar-sensitive were given aspartame as a substitute for sugar. Half the mothers were told their children were given sugar, half that their children were given aspartame. The mothers who thought their children had received sugar rated them as more hyperactive than the other children and were more critical of their behavior.[5]

Genetics

Attention disorders often run in families, so there are likely to be genetic influences. Studies indicate that 25 percent of the close relatives in the families of ADHD children also have ADHD, whereas the rate is about 5 percent in the general population.[6] Many studies of twins now show that a strong genetic influence exists in the disorder.[7]

Researchers continue to study the genetic contribution to ADHD and to identify the genes that cause a person to be susceptible to ADHD. Since its inception in 1999, the Attention-Deficit Hyperactivity Disorder Molecular Genetics Network has served as a way for researchers to share findings regarding possible genetic influences on ADHD.[8]

Recent Studies on Causes of ADHD

Some knowledge of the structure of the brain is helpful in understanding the research scientists are doing in searching for a physical basis for attention deficit hyperactivity disorder. One part of the brain that scientists have focused on in their search is the *frontal lobes of the cerebrum.* The frontal lobes allow us to solve problems, plan ahead, understand the behavior of others, and restrain our impulses. The two frontal lobes, the right and the left, communicate with each other through the *corpus callosum* (nerve fibers that connect the right and left frontal lobes).

The *basal ganglia* are the interconnected gray masses deep in the cerebral hemisphere that serve as the connection between the cerebrum and the *cerebellum* and, with the cerebellum, are responsible for motor coordination. The cerebellum is divided into three parts. The middle part is called the *vermis.*

All of these parts of the brain have been studied through the use of various methods for seeing into or imaging the brain. These methods include functional magnetic resonance imaging (fMRI) positron emission tomography

(PET), and single photon emission computed tomography (SPECT). The main or central psychological deficits in those with ADHD have been linked through these studies. By 2002 the researchers in the NIMH Child Psychiatry Branch had studied 152 boys and girls with ADHD, matched with 139 age- and gender-matched controls without ADHD. The children were scanned at least twice, some as many as four times over a decade. As a group, the ADHD children showed 3–4 percent smaller brain volumes in all regions—the frontal lobes, temporal gray matter, caudate nucleus, and cerebellum.

This study also showed that the ADHD children who were on medication had a white matter volume that did not differ from that of controls. Those never-medicated patients had an abnormally small volume of white matter. The white matter consists of fibers that establish long-distance connections between brain regions. It normally thickens as a child grows older and the brain matures.[9]

Although this long-term study used MRI to scan the children's brains, the researchers stressed that MRI remains a research tool and cannot be used to diagnose ADHD in any given child. This is true for other neurological methods of evaluating the brain, such as PET and SPECT.

DISORDERS THAT SOMETIMES ACCOMPANY ADHD

Learning Disabilities

Many children with ADHD—approximately 20 to 30 percent—also have a specific learning disability (LD).[10] In preschool years, these disabilities include difficulty in understanding certain sounds or words and/or difficulty in expressing oneself in words. In school age children, reading or spelling disabilities, writing disorders, and arithmetic disorders may appear. A type of reading disorder, *dyslexia*, is quite widespread. Reading disabilities affect up to 8 percent of elementary school children.

Tourette Syndrome

A very small proportion of people with ADHD have a neurological disorder called Tourette syndrome. People with Tourette syndrome have various nervous tics and repetitive mannerisms, such as eye blinks, facial twitches, or grimacing. Others may clear their throats frequently, snort, sniff, or bark out words. These behaviors can be controlled with medication. While very few children have this syndrome, many of the cases of Tourette syndrome have associated ADHD. In such cases, both disorders often require treatment that may include medications.

Oppositional Defiant Disorder

As many as one-third to one-half of all children with ADHD—mostly boys—have another condition, known as oppositional defiant disorder (ODD). These children are often defiant, stubborn, noncompliant, have outbursts of temper, or become belligerent. They argue with adults and refuse to obey.

Conduct Disorder

About 20 to 40 percent of ADHD children may eventually develop conduct disorder (CD), a more serious pattern of antisocial behavior. These children frequently lie or steal, fight with or bully others, and are at a real risk of getting into trouble at school or with the police. They violate the basic rights of other people, are aggressive toward people and/or animals, destroy property, break into people's homes, commit thefts, carry or use weapons, or engage in vandalism. These children or teens are at greater risk for substance use experimentation, and later dependence and abuse. They need immediate help.

Anxiety and Depression

Some children with ADHD often have co-occurring anxiety or depression. If the anxiety or depression is recognized and treated, the child will be better able to handle the problems that accompany ADHD. Conversely, effective treatment of ADHD can have a positive impact on anxiety as the child is better able to master academic tasks.

Bipolar Disorder

There are no accurate statistics on how many children with ADHD also have bipolar disorder. Differentiating between ADHD and bipolar disorder in childhood can be difficult. In its classic form, bipolar disorder is characterized by mood cycling between periods of intense highs and lows. But in children, bipolar disorder often seems to be a rather chronic mood dysregulation with a mixture of elation, depression, and irritability. Furthermore, there are some symptoms that can be present both in ADHD and bipolar disorder, such as a high level of energy and a reduced need for sleep. Of the symptoms differentiating children with ADHD from those with bipolar disorder, elated mood and grandiosity of the bipolar child are distinguishing characteristics.[11]

THE TREATMENT OF ADHD

Every family wants to determine what treatment will be most effective for their child. This question needs to be answered by each family in consultation with their health care professional. To help families make this important decision, the National Institute of Mental Health (NIMH) has funded many studies of treatments for ADHD and has conducted the most intensive study ever undertaken for evaluating the treatment of this disorder. This study is known as the Multimodal Treatment Study of Children with Attention Deficit Hyperactivity Disorder (MTA).[12] The NIMH is now conducting a clinical trial for younger children ages 3 to 5.5 years (Treatment of ADHD in Preschool-Age Children).

The Multimodal Treatment Study of Children with Attention Deficit Hyperactivity Disorder

The MTA study included 579 (95–98 at each of 6 treatment sites) elementary school boys and girls with ADHD, who were randomly assigned to one of four treatment programs: (1) medication management alone; (2) behavioral treatment alone; (3) a combination of both; or (4) routine community care. In each of the study sites, three groups were treated for the first 14 months in a specified protocol and the fourth group was referred for community treatment of the parents' choosing. All of the children were reassessed regularly throughout the study period. An essential part of the program was the cooperation of the schools, including principals and teachers. Both teachers and parents rated the children on hyperactivity, impulsivity, and inattention, and symptoms of anxiety and depression, as well as social skills.

The children in two groups (medication management alone and the combination treatment) were seen monthly for one half-hour at each medication visit. During the treatment visits, the prescribing physician spoke with the parent, met with the child, and sought to determine any concerns that the family might have regarding the medication or the child's ADHD-related difficulties. The physicians, in addition, sought input from the teachers on a monthly basis. The physicians in the medication-only group did not provide behavioral therapy but did advise the parents when necessary concerning any problems the child might have.

In the behavior treatment–only group, families met up to 35 times with a behavior therapist, mostly in group sessions. These therapists also made repeated visits to schools to consult with children's teachers and to supervise a special aide assigned to each child in the group. In addition, children attended a special 8-week summer treatment program where they worked on academic, social, and sports skills, and where intensive behavioral therapy was delivered to assist children in improving their behavior.

Children in the combined therapy group received both treatments, that is, all the same assistance that the medication-only group received, as well as all of the behavior therapy treatments.

In routine community care, the children saw the community-treatment doctor of their parents' choice one to two times per year for short periods of time. Also, the community-treatment doctor did not have any interaction with the teachers.

The results of the study indicated that long-term combination treatments and the medication-management alone were superior to intensive behavioral treatment and routine community treatment. And in some areas—anxiety, academic performance, oppositionality, parent-child relations, and social skills—the combined treatment was usually superior. Another advantage of combined treatment was that children could be successfully treated with lower doses of medicine, compared with the medication-only group.

Treatment of Attention Deficit Hyperactivity Disorder in Preschool-Age Children (PATS)

Because many children in the preschool years are diagnosed with ADHD and are given medication, it is important to know the safety and efficacy of such treatment. The NIMH is sponsoring an ongoing multi-site study, "Preschool ADHD Treatment Study" (PATS). It is the first major effort to examine the safety and efficacy of a stimulant, methylphenidate, for ADHD in this age group. The PATS study uses a randomized, placebo-controlled, double-blind design. Children ages 3 to 5 who have severe and persistent symptoms of ADHD that impair their functioning are eligible for this study. To avoid using medications at such an early age, all children who enter the study are first treated with behavioral therapy. Only children who do not show sufficient improvement with behavior therapy are considered for the medication part of the study. The study is being conducted at New York State Psychiatric Institute, Duke University, Johns Hopkins University, New York University, the University of California at Los Angeles, and the University of California at Irvine. Enrollment in the study will total 165 children.

Which Treatment Should My Child Have?

For children with ADHD, no single treatment is the answer for every child. A child may sometimes have undesirable side effects to a medication that would make that particular treatment unacceptable. And if a child with ADHD also has anxiety or depression, a treatment combining medication and behavioral therapy might be best. Each child's needs and personal history must be carefully considered.

Medications

For decades, medications have been used to treat the symptoms of ADHD.

The medications that seem to be the most effective are a class of drugs known as stimulants. Following is a list of the stimulants, their trade (or

Trade Name	Generic Name	Approved Age
Adderall	amphetamine	3 and older
Concerta	methylphenidate (long acting)	6 and older
Cylert*	pemoline	6 and older
Dexedrine	dextroamphetamine	3 and older
Dextrostat	dextroamphetamine	3 and older
Focalin	dexmethylphenidate	6 and older
Metadate ER	methylphenidate (extended release)	6 and older
Metadate CD	methylphenidate (extended release)	6 and older
Ritalin	methylphenidate	6 and older
Ritalin SR	methylphenidate (extended release)	6 and older
Ritalin LA	methylphenidate (long acting)	6 and older

* Because of its potential for serious side effects affecting the liver, Cylert should not ordinarily be considered as first-line drug therapy for ADHD.

brand) names, and their generic names. "Approved age" means that the drug has been tested and found safe and effective in children of that age.

The U.S. Food and Drug Administration (FDA) recently approved a medication for ADHD that is not a stimulant. The medication, Strattera®, or atomoxetine, works on the neurotransmitter norepinephrine, whereas the stimulants primarily work on dopamine. Both of these neurotransmitters are believed to play a role in ADHD. More studies will need to be done to contrast Strattera with the medications already available, but the evidence to date indicates that over 70 percent of children with ADHD given Strattera manifest significant improvement in their symptoms.

Some people get better results from one medication, some from another. It is important to work with the prescribing physician to find the right medication and the right dosage. For many people, the stimulants dramatically reduce their hyperactivity and impulsivity and improve their ability to focus, work, and learn. The medications may also improve physical coordination, such as that needed in handwriting and in sports.

The stimulant drugs, when used with medical supervision, are usually considered quite safe. Stimulants do not make the child feel "high," although some children say they feel different or funny. Such changes are usually very minor. Although some parents worry that their child may become addicted to the medication, to date there is no convincing evidence that stimulant medications, when used for treatment of ADHD, cause drug abuse or dependence. A review of all long-term studies on stimulant medication and substance abuse, conducted by researchers at Massachusetts General Hospital and

Harvard Medical School, found that teenagers with ADHD who remained on their medication during the teen years had a lower likelihood of substance use or abuse than did ADHD adolescents who were not taking medications.[13]

The stimulant drugs come in long- and short-term forms. The newer sustained-release stimulants can be taken before school and are long-lasting so that the child does not need to go to the school nurse every day for a pill. The doctor can discuss with the parents the child's needs and decide which preparation to use and whether the child needs to take the medicine during school hours only or in the evening and on weekends too.

If the child does not show symptom improvement after taking a medication for a week, the doctor may try adjusting the dosage. If there is still no improvement, the child may be switched to another medication. About one out of ten children is not helped by a stimulant medication. Other types of medication may be used if stimulants don't work or if the ADHD occurs with another disorder. Antidepressants and other medications can help control accompanying depression or anxiety.

Sometimes the doctor may prescribe for a young child a medication that has been approved by the FDA for use in adults or older children. This use of the medication is called "off label." Many of the newer medications that are proving helpful for child mental disorders are prescribed off label because only a few of them have been systematically studied for safety and efficacy in children. Medications that have not undergone such testing are dispensed with the statement that "safety and efficacy have not been established in pediatric patients."

Side Effects of the Medications

Most side effects of the stimulant medications are minor and are usually related to the dosage of the medication being taken. Higher doses produce more side effects. The most common side effects are decreased appetite, insomnia, increased anxiety, and/or irritability. Some children report mild stomachaches or headaches.

Appetite seems to fluctuate, usually being low during the middle of the day and more normal by suppertime. Adequate amounts of food that is nutritional should be available for the child, especially at peak appetite times.

If the child has difficulty falling asleep, several options may be tried—a lower dosage of the stimulant, giving the stimulant earlier in the day, discontinuing the afternoon or evening dosage, or giving an adjunct medication such as a low-dosage antidepressant or clonidine. A few children develop tics during treatment. These can often be lessened by changing the medication dosage. A very few children cannot tolerate any stimulant, no matter how low the dosage. In such cases, the child is often given an antidepressant instead of the stimulant.

When a child's schoolwork and behavior improve soon after starting medication, the child, parents, and teachers tend to applaud the drug for causing the sudden changes. Unfortunately, when people see such immediate improvement, they often think medication is all that's needed. But medications don't cure ADHD; they only control the symptoms on the day they are taken. Although the medications help the child pay better attention and complete school work, they can't increase knowledge or improve academic skills. The medications help the child to use those skills he or she already possesses.

Behavioral therapy, emotional counseling, and practical support will help ADHD children cope with everyday problems and feel better about themselves.

Facts to Remember About Medication for ADHD

- Medications for ADHD help many children focus and be more successful at school, home, and play. Avoiding negative experiences now may actually help prevent addictions and other emotional problems later.
- About 80 percent of children who need medication for ADHD still need it as teenagers. Over 50 percent need medication as adults.

Medication for the Child with Both ADHD and Bipolar Disorder

Since a child with bipolar disorder will probably be prescribed a mood stabilizer such as lithium or Depakote®, the doctor will carefully consider whether the child should take one of the medications usually prescribed for ADHD. If a stimulant medication is prescribed, it may be given in a lower dosage than usual.

THE FAMILY AND THE ADHD CHILD

Medication can help the ADHD child in everyday life. He or she may be better able to control some of the behavior problems that have led to trouble with parents and siblings. But it takes time to undo the frustration, blame, and anger that may have gone on for so long. Both parents and children may need special help to develop techniques for managing the patterns of behavior. In such cases, mental health professionals can counsel the child and the family, helping them to develop new skills, attitudes, and ways of relating to each other. In individual counseling, the therapist helps children with ADHD learn to feel better about themselves. The therapist can also help them to identify and build on their strengths, cope with daily problems, and control their attention and aggression. Sometimes only the child with ADHD needs counseling support. But in many cases, because the problem affects the family as a whole, the entire family may need help. The therapist assists the family in finding better ways to handle the disruptive behaviors and promote change. If the child is young, most of the therapist's work is with the parents, teaching them techniques for coping with and improving their child's behavior.

Several intervention approaches are available. Knowing something about the various types of interventions makes it easier for families to choose a therapist that is right for their needs.

Psychotherapy works to help people with ADHD to like and accept themselves despite their disorder. It does not address the symptoms or underlying causes of the disorder. In psychotherapy, patients talk with the therapist about upsetting thoughts and feelings, explore self-defeating patterns of behavior, and learn alternative ways to handle their emotions. As they talk, the therapist tries to help them understand how they can change or better cope with their disorder.

Behavioral therapy (BT) helps people develop more effective ways to work on immediate issues. Rather than helping the child understand his or her feelings and actions, it helps directly in changing their thinking and coping and thus may lead to changes in behavior. The support might be practical assistance, like help in organizing tasks or schoolwork or dealing with emotionally charged events. Or the support might be in self-monitoring one's own behavior and giving self-praise or rewards for acting in a desired way such as controlling anger or thinking before acting.

Social skills training can also help children learn new behaviors. In social skills training, the therapist discusses and models appropriate behaviors important in developing and maintaining social relationships, like waiting for a turn, sharing toys, asking for help, or responding to teasing, then gives children a chance to practice. For example, a child might learn to "read" other people's facial expression and tone of voice in order to respond appropriately. Social skills training helps the child to develop better ways to play and work with other children.

Support groups help parents connect with other people who have similar problems and concerns with their ADHD children. Members of support groups often meet on a regular basis (such as monthly) to hear lectures from experts on ADHD, share frustrations and successes, and obtain referrals to qualified specialists and information about what works. There is strength in numbers, and sharing experiences with others who have similar problems helps people know that they aren't alone. National organizations are listed at the end of this document.

Parenting skills training, offered by therapists or in special classes, gives parents tools and techniques for managing their child's behavior. One such technique is the use of token or point systems for immediately rewarding good behavior or work. Another is the use of "time-out" or isolation to a chair or bedroom when the child becomes too unruly or out of control. During time-outs, the child is removed from the agitating situation and sits alone quietly for a short time to calm down. Parents may also be taught to give the child "quality time" each day, in which they share a pleasurable or relaxing activity. During this time together, the parent looks for opportunities to notice and point out what the child does well, and praise his or her strengths and abilities.

This system of rewards and penalties can be an effective way to modify a child's behavior. The parents (or teacher) identify a few desirable behaviors that they want to encourage in the child—such as asking for a toy instead of grabbing it, or completing a simple task. The child is told exactly what is expected in order to earn the reward. The child receives the reward when he performs the desired behavior and a mild penalty when he doesn't. A reward can be small, perhaps a token that can be exchanged for special privileges, but it should be something the child wants and is eager to earn. The penalty might be removal of a token or a brief time-out. *Make an effort to find your child being good.* The goal, over time, is to help children learn to control their own behavior and to choose the more desired behavior. The technique works well with all children, although children with ADHD may need more frequent rewards.

In addition, parents may learn to structure situations in ways that will allow their child to succeed. This may include allowing only one or two playmates at a time, so that their child doesn't get overstimulated. Or if their child has trouble completing tasks, they may learn to help the child divide a large task into small steps, then praise the child as each step is completed. Regardless of the specific technique parents may use to modify their child's behavior, some general principles appear to be useful for most children with ADHD. These include providing more frequent and immediate feedback (including rewards and punishment), setting up more structure in advance of potential problem situations, and providing greater supervision and encouragement to children with ADHD in relatively unrewarding or tedious situations.

Parents may also learn to use stress management methods, such as meditation, relaxation techniques, and exercise, to increase their own tolerance for frustration so that they can respond more calmly to their child's behavior.

Some Simple Behavioral Interventions

Children with ADHD may need help in organizing. Therefore:

- **Schedule.** Have the same routine every day, from wake-up time to bedtime. The schedule should include homework time and playtime (including outdoor recreation and indoor activities such as computer games). Have the schedule on the refrigerator or a bulletin board in the kitchen. If a schedule change must be made, make it as far in advance as possible.
- **Organize needed everyday items.** Have a place for everything and keep everything in its place. This includes clothing, backpacks, and school supplies.
- **Use homework and notebook organizers.** Stress the importance of writing down assignments and bringing home needed books.

Children with ADHD need consistent rules that they can understand and follow. If rules are followed, give small rewards. Children with ADHD often receive, and expect, criticism. Look for good behavior and praise it.

Your ADHD Child and School

You are your child's best advocate. To be a good advocate for your child, learn as much as you can about ADHD and how it affects your child at home, in school, and in social situations.

If your child has shown symptoms of ADHD from an early age and has been evaluated, diagnosed, and treated with either behavior modification or medication or a combination of both, when your child enters the school system, let his or her teachers know. They will be better prepared to help the child come into this new world away from home.

If your child enters school and experiences difficulties that lead you to suspect that he or she has ADHD, you can either seek the services of an outside professional or you can ask the local school district to conduct an evaluation. Some parents prefer to go to a professional of their own choice. But it is the school's obligation to evaluate children that they suspect have ADHD or some other disability that is affecting not only their academic work but their interactions with classmates and teachers.

If you feel that your child has ADHD and isn't learning in school as he or she should, you should find out just who in the school system you should contact. Your child's teacher should be able to help you with this information. Then you can request—in writing—that the school system evaluate your child.

The letter should include the date, your and your child's names, and the reason for requesting an evaluation. Keep a copy of the letter in your own files.

Until the last few years, many school systems were reluctant to evaluate a child with ADHD. But recent laws have made clear the school's obligation to the child suspected of having ADHD that is affecting adversely his or her performance in school. If the school persists in refusing to evaluate your child, you can either get a private evaluation or enlist some help in negotiating with the school. Help is often as close as a local parent group. Each state has a Parent Training and Information (PTI) center as well as a Protection and Advocacy (P&A) agency. (For information on the law and on the PTI and P&A, see the section on support groups and organizations at the end of this document.)

Once your child has been diagnosed with ADHD and qualifies for special education services, the school, working with you, must assess the child's strengths and weaknesses and design an Individualized Educational Program (IEP). You should be able periodically to review and approve your child's IEP. Each school year brings a new teacher and new schoolwork, a transition that can be quite difficult for the child with ADHD. Your child needs lots of support and encouragement at this time.

Never forget the cardinal rule—**you are your child's best advocate**.

Your Teenager with ADHD

Your child with ADHD has successfully navigated the early school years and is beginning his or her journey through middle school and high school. Although your child has been periodically evaluated through the years, this is a good time to have a complete reevaluation of your child's health.

The teen years are challenging for most children; for the child with ADHD these years are doubly hard. All the adolescent problems—peer pressure, the fear of failure in both school and socially, low self-esteem—are harder for the ADHD child to handle. The desire to be independent, to try new and forbidden things—alcohol, drugs, and sexual activity—can lead to unforeseen consequences. The rules that once were, for the most part, followed, are often now flouted. Parents may not agree with each other on how the teenager's behavior should be handled.

Now, more than ever, rules should be straightforward and easy to understand. Communication between the adolescent and parents can help the teenager to know the reasons for each rule. When a rule is set, it should be clear *why* the rule is set. Sometimes it helps to have a chart, posted usually in the kitchen, that lists all household rules and all rules for outside the home (social and school). Another chart could list household chores with space to check off a chore once it is done.

When rules are broken—and they will be—respond to this inappropriate behavior as calmly and matter-of-factly as possible. Use punishment sparingly. Even with teens, a time-out can work. Impulsivity and hot temper often accompany ADHD. A short time alone can help.

As the teenager spends more time away from home, there will be demands for a later curfew and the use of the car. Listen to your child's request, give reasons for your opinion and listen to his or her opinion, and negotiate. *Communication, negotiation, and compromise* will prove helpful.

Your Teenager and the Car

Teenagers, especially boys, begin talking about driving by the time they are 15. In some states, a learner's permit is available at 15 and a driver's license at 16. Statistics show that 16-year-old drivers have more accidents per driving mile than any other age. In the year 2000, 18 percent of those who died in speed-related crashes were youth ages 15 to 19. Sixty-six percent of these youth were not wearing safety belts. Youth with ADHD, in their first 2 to 5 years of driving, have nearly four times as many automobile accidents, are more likely to cause bodily injury in accidents, and have three times as many citations for speeding as the young drivers without ADHD.[14]

Most states, after looking at the statistics for automobile accidents involving teenage drivers, have begun to use a graduated driver licensing system (GDL). This system eases young drivers onto the roads by a slow progression of exposure to more difficult driving experiences. The program, as developed by the National Highway Traffic Safety Administration and the American Association of Motor Vehicle Administrators, consists of three stages: learner's permit, intermediate (provisional) license, and full licensure. Drivers must demonstrate responsible driving behavior at each stage before advancing to the next level. During the learner's permit stage, a licensed adult must be in the car at all times.[15] This period of time will give the learner a chance to practice, practice, practice. The more your child drives, the more efficient he or she will become. The sense of accomplishment the teenager with ADHD will feel when the coveted license is finally in his or her hands will make all the time and effort involved worthwhile.

Note: The State Legislative Fact Sheets—Graduated Driver Licensing System can be found at web site http://www.nhtsa.dot.gov/people/outreach/safesobr/21qp/html/fact_sheets/Graduated_Driver.html, or it can be ordered from NHTSA Headquarters, Traffic Safety Programs, ATTN:

NTS-32, 400 Seventh Street, S.W., Washington, DC 20590; telephone 202-366-6948.

ATTENTION DEFICIT HYPERACTIVITY DISORDER IN ADULTS

Attention deficit hyperactivity disorder is a highly publicized childhood disorder that affects approximately 3 percent to 5 percent of all children. What is much less well known is the probability that, of children who have ADHD, many will still have it as adults. Several studies done in recent years estimate that between 30 percent and 70 percent of children with ADHD continue to exhibit symptoms in the adult years.[16]

The first studies on adults who were never diagnosed as children as having ADHD, but showed symptoms as adults, were done in the late 1970s by Drs. Paul Wender, Frederick Reimherr, and David Wood. These symptomatic adults were retrospectively diagnosed with ADHD after the researchers' interviews with their parents. The researchers developed clinical criteria for the diagnosis of adult ADHD (the Utah Criteria), which combined past history of ADHD with current evidence of ADHD behaviors.[17] Other diagnostic assessments are now available; among them are the widely used Conners Rating Scale and the Brown Attention Deficit Disorder Scale.

Typically, adults with ADHD are unaware that they have this disorder—they often just feel that it's impossible to get organized, to stick to a job, to keep an appointment. The everyday tasks of getting up, getting dressed and ready for the day's work, getting to work on time, and being productive on the job can be major challenges for the ADHD adult.

Diagnosing ADHD in an Adult

Diagnosing an adult with ADHD is not easy. Many times, when a child is diagnosed with the disorder, a parent will recognize that he or she has many of the same symptoms the child has and, for the first time, will begin to understand some of the traits that have given him or her trouble for years—distractibility, impulsivity, restlessness. Other adults will seek professional help for depression or anxiety and will find out that the root cause of some of their emotional problems is ADHD. They may have a history of school failures or problems at work. Often they have been involved in frequent automobile accidents.

To be diagnosed with ADHD, an adult must have childhood-onset, persistent, and current symptoms.[18] The accuracy of the diagnosis of adult ADHD is of utmost importance and should be made by a clinician with expertise in the area of attention dysfunction. For an accurate diagnosis, a history of the patient's childhood behavior, together with an interview with his or her life partner, a parent, a close friend, or an other close associate, will be needed. A physical examination and psychological tests should also be given. Comorbidity with other conditions may exist such as specific learning disabilities, anxiety, or affective disorders.

A correct diagnosis of ADHD can bring a sense of relief. The individual has brought into adulthood many negative perceptions of himself that may have led to low esteem. Now he can begin to understand why he has some of his problems and can begin to face them. This may mean, not only treatment for ADHD but also psychotherapy that can help him cope with the anger he feels about the failure to diagnose the disorder when he was younger.

Treatment of ADHD in an Adult

Medications. As with children, if adults take a medication for ADHD, they often start with a stimulant medication. The stimulant medications affect the regulation of two neurotransmitters, norepinephrine and dopamine. The newest medication approved for ADHD by the FDA, atomoxetine (Strattera®), has been tested in controlled studies in both children and adults and has been found to be effective.[19]

Antidepressants are considered a second choice for treatment of adults with ADHD. The older antidepressants, the tricyclics, are sometimes used because they, like the stimulants, affect norepinephrine and dopamine. Venlafaxine (Effexor®), a newer antidepressant, is also used for its effect on norepinephrine. Bupropion (Wellbutrin®), an antidepressant with an indirect effect on the neurotransmitter dopamine, has been useful in clinical trials on the treatment of ADHD in both children and adults. It has the added attraction of being useful in reducing cigarette smoking.

In prescribing for an adult, special considerations are made. The adult may need less of the medication for his weight. A medication may have a longer "half-life" in an adult. The adult may take other medications for physical problems such as diabetes or high blood pressure. Often the adult is also taking a medication for anxiety or depression. All of these variables must be taken into account before a medication is prescribed.

Education and psychotherapy. Although medication gives needed support, the individual must succeed on his own. To help in this struggle, both "psychoeducation" and individual psychotherapy can be helpful. A professional coach can help the ADHD adult learn how to organize his life by using "props"—a large calendar posted where it will be seen in the morning, date books, lists, reminder notes, and have a special place for keys, bills, and the paperwork of everyday life. Tasks can be organized into sections, so that completion of each part can give a sense of accomplishment. Above all, ADHD adults should learn as much as they can about their disorder.

Psychotherapy can be a useful adjunct to medication and education. First, just remembering to keep an appointment with the therapist is a step toward keeping to a routine. Therapy can help change a long-standing poor self-image by examining the experiences that produced it. The therapist can encourage the ADHD patient to adjust to changes brought into his life by treatment—the perceived loss of impulsivity and love of risk-taking, the new sensation of thinking before acting. As the patient begins to have small successes in his new ability to bring organization out of the complexities of his or her life, he or she can begin to appreciate the characteristics of ADHD that are positive—boundless energy, warmth, and enthusiasm.

REFERENCES AND RESOURCE BOOKS

References

1. Still GF. Some abnormal psychical conditions in children: the Goulstonian lectures. *Lancet*, 1902; 1:1008–1012.
2. DSM-IV-TR workgroup. *The Diagnostic and Statistical Manual of Mental Disorders*, Fourth Edition, Text Revision. Washington, DC: American Psychiatric Association.
3. Consensus Development Panel. *Defined Diets and Childhood Hyperactivity*. National Institutes of Health Consensus Development Conference Summary, Volume 4, Number 3, 1982.
4. Wolraich M, Milich R, Stumbo P, Schultz F. The effects of sucrose ingestion on the behavior of hyperactive boys. *Pediatrics*, 1985; 106: 657–682.
5. Hoover DW, Milich R. Effects of sugar ingestion expectancies on mother-child interaction. *Journal of Abnormal Child Psychology*, 1994; 22: 501–515.
6. Biederman J, Faraone SV, Keenan K, Knee D, Tsuang MF. Family-genetic and psychosocial risk factors in DSM-III attention deficit disorder. *Journal of the American Academy of Child and Adolescent Psychiatry*, 1990; 29(4): 526–533.
7. Faraone SV, Biederman J. Neurobiology of attention-deficit hyperactivity disorder. *Biological Psychiatry*, 1998; 44: 951–958.
8. The ADHD Molecular Genetics Network. Report from the third international meeting of the attention-deficit hyperactivity disorder molecular genetics network. *American Journal of Medical Genetics*, 2002; 114:272–277.
9. Castellanos FX, Lee PP, Sharp W, Jeffries NO, Greenstein DK, Clasen LS, Blumenthal JD, James RS, Ebens CI, Walter JM, Zijdenbos A, Evans AC, Giedd JN, Rapoport JL. Developmental trajectories of brain volume abnormalities in children and adolescents with attention-deficit/hyperactivity disorder. *Journal of the American Medical Association*, 2002; 288(14): 1740–1748.

10. Wender PH. *ADHD: Attention-Deficit Hyperactivity Disorder in Children and Adults.* Oxford University Press, 2002, p. 9.

11. Geller B, Williams M, Zimerman B, Frazier J, Beringer L, Warner KL. Prepubertal and early adolescent bipolarity differentiate from ADHD by manic symptoms, grandiose delusions, ultra-rapid or ultradian cycling. *Journal of Affective Disorders*; 1998, 51:81–91.

12. The MTA Cooperative Group. A 14-month randomized clinical trial of treatment strategies for attention-deficit hyperactivity disorder (ADHD). *Archives of General Psychiatry*, 1999; 56:1073–1086.

13. Wilens TC, Faraone, SV, Biederman J, Gunawardene S. Does stimulant therapy of attention-deficit/hyperactivity disorder beget later substance abuse? A meta-analytic review of the literature. *Pediatrics*, 2003; 111(1): 179–185.

14. Barkley RA. *Taking Charge of ADHD.* New York: The Guilford Press, 2000, p. 21.

15. U.S. Department of Transportation, National Highway Traffic Safety Administration. *State Legislative Fact Sheet*, April 2002.

16. Silver LB. Attention-deficit hyperactivity disorder in adult life. *Child and Adolescent Psychiatric Clinics of North America*, 2000; 9(3): 411–523.

17. Wender PH. Pharmacotherapy of attention-deficit/hyperactivity in adults. *Journal of Clinical Psychiatry*, 1998; 59 (supplement 7): 76–79.

18. Wilens TE, Biederman J, Spencer TJ. Attention deficit/hyperactivity disorder across the lifespan. *Annual Review of Medicine*, 2002; 53:113–131.

19. *Attention Deficit Disorder in Adults.* Harvard Mental Health Letter, 2002; 19(5): 3–6.

Resource Books

The following books were helpful resources in the writing of this document. Many other informative books can be found at any good bookstore, on a website that offers books for sale, or from the ADD Warehouse catalog.

Taking Charge of ADHD, by Russell A. Barkley, PhD. New York: The Guilford Press, 2000.

ADHD: Attention-Deficit Hyperactivity Disorder in Children and Adults, by Paul H. Wender, MD. Oxford University Press, 2002.

Straight Talk about Psychiatric Medications for Kids, by Timothy E. Wilens, MD. New York: The Guilford Press, 1999.

Glossary

American Academy of Child and Adolescent Psychiatry (AACAP) is an organization composed of over 7,500 child and adolescent psychiatrists and other interested physicians. Members of the AACAP research, evaluate, diagnose, and treat psychiatric disorders in children and adolescents.

American Academy of Pediatrics (AAP) is an organization of 60,000 pediatricians committed to the attainment of optimal physical, mental, and social health and well-being for all infants, children, adolescents, and young adults.

American Psychiatric Association (APA) is an organization of over 38,000 U.S. and international member physicians working together to ensure humane care and effective treatment for all persons with mental disorders, including mental retardation and substance related disorders. The vision of APA is a society that has available, accessible quality psychiatric diagnosis and treatment.

Bipolar Disorder: Children and teenagers with bipolar disorder have manic and/or depressive symptoms. Some may have mostly depression and others a combination of manic and depressive symptoms. Highs may alternate with lows. Manic symptoms include severe changes in mood: unusually happy or silly, or very irritable, angry, agitated, or aggressive. Depressive symptoms include irritability, depressed mood, persistent sadness, frequent crying, and thoughts about suicide.

Child and Adolescent Psychiatrist: A physician who specializes in the diagnosis and the treatment of disorders of thinking, feeling, or behavior affecting children, adolescents, and their families. The child and adolescent psychiatrist uses knowledge of biological, psychological, and social factors in working with patients. Child and adolescent psychiatric training requires four years of medical school; at least three years of approved residency training in medicine, neurology, and general psychiatry with adults; and two years of additional specialized training in psychiatric work with children, adolescents, and their families in a residency in child and adolescent psychiatry.

Comorbid is a condition that coexists with a separate medical condition. Many comorbid conditions commonly occur together (e.g., ADHD and tic disorders, depression and anxiety).

Conduct Disorder refers to a group of behavioral and emotional problems in youngsters. Children and adolescents with this disorder have great difficulty following rules and behaving in a socially acceptable way. They are often viewed by other children, adults, and social agencies as "bad" or delinquent rather than mentally ill. Many factors may contribute to a child developing conduct disorder, including brain damage, child abuse, genetic vulnerability, school failure, and traumatic life experiences.

Criterion: Singular form of criteria.

Diagnostic Criteria are a uniform system of diagnosis for developmental and mental health disorders; features of the condition are summarized as criteria that are expected to be present. The goal is to fully describe the essential components that differentiate a particular condition (e.g., ADHD) from another (e.g., specific language impairment).

Diagnostic and Statistical Manual (DSM) is the standard classification of mental disorders used by mental health professionals in the U.S. It is intended to be applicable in a wide array of contexts and used by clinicians and researchers of many different orientations (e.g., biological, psychodynamic, cognitive, behavioral, interpersonal, family/systems). The *Diagnostic and Statistical Manual of Mental Disorders, Fourth Edition (DSM-IV)* has been designed for use across clinical settings (inpatient, outpatient, partial hospital, consultation-liaison, clinic, private practice, and primary care) with community populations. It is also a necessary tool for collecting and communicating accurate public health statistics.

Executive Functioning is the ability to maintain an appropriate problem-solving set for reaching a future goal. The term executive function refers to many behaviors and cognitive processes, such as self-regulation, flexibility, and planning and organization of behavior, and is considered to overlap with attention.

Food and Drug Association (FDA) is an agency within the Department of Health and Human Services (HHS), the U.S. government's principal agency for protecting the health of all Americans and providing essential human services. In support of the agency's mission to promote and protect the public health, the FDA focuses on three goals: 1) improve patient and consumer safety, 2) increase access to new medical and food products, and 3) improve the quality and safety of manufactured products.

Genes are separate areas on a chromosome that code for a protein that has a special function in the body. If the gene is changed in some way, the function of that protein can be affected, resulting in a change that can cause problems for the body, depending on which gene is involved and how much the gene is altered.

Hyperactivity is being on the move, walking, running, or climbing around when others are seated; a hyperactive person talks when others are talking.

Impulsivity is acting quickly without thinking first.

Inattention is daydreaming or being in another world.

Learning Disability usually involves children with a normal range of intelligence. Learning disabilities affect at least one in ten schoolchildren. It is believed that learning disabilities are caused by a difficulty with the nervous system that affects receiving, processing, or communicating information. Signs of learning disabilities include 1) difficulty understanding and following instructions; 2) trouble remembering what someone just told the person; 3) failing to master reading, spelling, writing, and/or math skills, and thus failure in these areas; and 4) difficulty distinguishing right from left, or difficulty identifying words or a tendency to reverse letters, words, or numbers (for example, confusing 25 with 52, "b" with "d," or "on" with "no").

Major Depressive Disorder is an illness in which the feelings of depression persist and interfere with a child or adolescent's ability to function. Signs of depression include 1) frequent sadness, tearfulness, and crying; 2) decreased interest in activities or inability to enjoy previously favorite activities; 3) hopelessness; 4) persistent boredom, and low energy; 5) social isolation, and poor communication; and 6) low self-esteem and guilt. Depression is a real illness that requires professional help. Early diagnosis and treatment are essential for depressed children.

National Institute on Drug Abuse (NIDA) is the federal focal point for research on drug abuse and addiction, and is part of the National Institutes of Health, Department of Health and Human Services. NIDA addresses the most fundamental and essential questions about drug abuse, from detecting and responding to emerging drug abuse trends and understanding how drugs work in the brain and body to developing and testing new treatment and prevention approaches.

National Institute of Mental Health (NIMH) is the largest scientific organization in the world dedicated to research focused on the understanding, treatment, and prevention of mental disorders and the promotion of mental health.

Neuropsychological Testing is an evaluation of a child to determine his or her needs for special education or related services. The evaluation may include psychological and educational testing, a speech and language evaluation, occupational therapy assessment, and a behavioral analysis. The results of the evaluation determine a child's eligibility to receive a range of services under the applicable law. After the evaluation, an individualized education program (IEP) is developed. Examples of categories of services in IEPs include occupational therapy, physical therapy, speech and language therapy, and/or the provision of a classroom aide.

Oppositional Defiant Disorder (ODD) is an ongoing pattern of uncooperative, defiant, and hostile behavior toward authority figures that seriously interferes with the youngster's day-to-day functioning. Symptoms of ODD include 1) frequent temper tantrums, 2) excessive arguing with adults, and 3) active defiance and refusal to comply with adult requests and rules.

Primary Care Provider (PCP) is a health care professional who sees a patient on a regular basis. The PCP for most children is a pediatrician, family practitioner, or other professional (nurse practitioner or physician's assistant working in collaboration with a physician).

Tics occur when a part of the body moves repeatedly, quickly, suddenly, and uncontrollably. Tics can occur in any body part, such as the face, shoulders, hands, or legs. They can be stopped voluntarily for brief periods. Sounds that are made involuntarily (such as throat clearing) are called vocal tics. Most tics are mild and hardly noticeable. However, in some cases they are frequent and severe and can affect many areas of a child's life.

References

BOOKS

Adler L., and J. Cohen. 2004. Diagnosis and evaluation of adults with attention-deficit/ hyperactivity disorder. *Psychiatry Clin. North Am.* 27:187–201.

American Academy of Child and Adolescent Psychiatry (AACAP). 2007. *Practice Parameter for the Assessment and Treatment of Children and Adolescents with ADHD.* Washington, DC: AACAP.

American Psychiatric Association. 2000. *Diagnostic and Statistical Manual of Mental Disorders.* 4th ed, text revision. Washington, DC: American Psychiatric Association.

Anthony, E. J. 1973. A psychodynamic model of minimal brain dysfunction. *Ann. N. Y. Acad. Sci.* 205:52–60.

Banerjee, T. D., F. Middleton, and S. V. Faraone. 2007. Environmental risk factors for attention-deficit hyperactivity disorder. *Acta Paediatr.* 96:1269–74.

Barkley, R. A., K. R. Murphy, G. J. Dupaul, and T. Bush. 2002. Driving in young adults with attention deficit hyperactivity disorder: Knowledge, performance, adverse outcomes, and the role of executive functioning. *J. Int. Neuropsychol. Soc.* 8:655–72.

Benton, A. L. 1973. Minimal brain dysfunction from a neuropsychological point of view. *Ann. N. Y. Acad. Sci.* 205:29–37.

Biederman, J. 2004. Impact of comorbidity in adults with attention-deficit/hyperactivity disorder. *J. Clin. Psychiatry* 65(Suppl 3):3–7.

Biederman, J., C. R. Petty, T. E. Wilens, M. G. Fraire, C. A. Purcell, E. Mick, M. C. Monuteaux, and S. V. Faraone. 2008. Familial risk analyses of attention deficit hyperactivity disorder and substance use disorders. *Am. J. Psychiatry* 165:107–15.

Biederman, J., E. Mick, and S. V. Faraone. 2000. Age-dependent decline of symptoms of attention deficit hyperactivity disorder: Impact of remission definition and symptom type. *Am. J. Psychiatry* 157:816–8.

Biederman, J., M. C. Monuteaux, E. Mick, T. Spencer, T. E. Wilens, J. M. Silva, L. E. Snyder, and S. V. Faraone. 2006. Young adult outcome of attention deficit hyperactivity disorder: A controlled 10-year follow-up study. *Psychol. Med.* 36:167–79.

Biederman, J. and S. V. Faraone. 2004. ADHD: A worldwide concern. *J. Nerv. Ment. Dis.* 192:453–45.

Biederman, J., and S. V. Faraone. 2005. Attention-deficit hyperactivity disorder (diagnosis and treatment). *Lancet* 366:237–48.

Biederman, J., S. V. Faraone, T. J. Spencer, T. Wilens, D. Norman, K. A. Lapey, E. Mick, B. K. Lehman, and A. Doyle. 1993. Patterns of psychiatric comorbidity, cognition, and psychosocial functioning in adults with attention deficit hyperactivity disorder. *Am. J. Psychiatry* 150:1792–8.

Biederman, J., S. V. Faraone, T. J. Spencer, E. Mick, M. C. Monuteaux, and M. Aleardi. 2006. Functional impairments in adults with self-reports of diagnosed ADHD: A controlled study of 1001 adults in the community. *J. Clin. Psychiatry* 67:524–40.

Biederman, J., T. Wilens, E. Mick, S. V. Faraone, W. Weber, S. Curtis, A. Thornell, K. Pfister, J. G. Jetton, and J. Soriano. 1997. Is ADHD a risk factor for psychoactive substance use disorders? Findings from a four-year prospective follow-up study. *J. Am. Acad. Child. Adolesc. Psychiatry* 36:21–9.

Biederman, J., T. Wilens, E. Mick, S. Milberger, T. J. Spencer, and S. V. Faraone. 1995. Psychoactive substance use disorders in adults with attention deficit hyperactivity disorder (ADHD): Effects of ADHD and psychiatric comorbidity. *Am. J. Psychiatry* 152:1652–8.

Biederman, J., T. Wilens, E. Mick, T. Spencer, and S. V. Faraone. 1999. Pharmacotherapy of attention-deficit/hyperactivity disorder reduces risk for substance use disorder. *Pediatrics* 104:e20.

Bush, G., J. A. Frazier, S. L. Rauch, L. J. Seidman, P. J. Whalen, M. A. Jenike, B. R. Rosen, and J. Biederman. 1999. Anterior cingulate cortex dysfunction in attention-deficit/hyperactivity disorder revealed by fMRI and the counting stroop. *Biol. Psychiatry* 145:1542–52.

Cantwell, D. P.1972. Psychiatric illness in the families of hyperactive children. *Arch. Gen. Psychiatry* 27:414–17.

Casey, B. J., J. N. Epstein, J. Buhle, C. Liston, M. C. Davidson, S. T. Tonev, J. Spicer, S. Niogi, A. J. Millner, A. Reiss, A. Garrett, S. P. Hinshaw, L. L. Greenhill, K. M. Shafritz, A. Vitolo, L. A. Kotler, M. A. Jarrett, and G. Glover. 2007. Frontostriatal connectivity and its role in cognitive control in parent-child dyads with ADHD. *Am. J. Psychiatry* 164:1729–36.

Castellanos, F. X., P. P. Lee, W. Sharp, N. O. Jeffries, D. K. Greenstein, L. S. Clasen, J. D. Blumenthal, R. S. James, C. L. Ebens, J. M. Walter, A. Zijdenbos, A. C. Evans, J. N. Giedd, and J. L. Rapoport. 2002. Developmental trajectories of brain volume abnormalities in children and adolescents with attention-deficit/hyperactivity disorder. *JAMA* 288:1740–8.

Centers for Disease Control. 2005. Mental health in the United States: Prevalence of diagnosis and medication treatment for attention-deficit/hyperactivity disorder— United States, 2003. *MMWR. Morb. Mortal. Wkly. Rep.* 54:842–7.

Clements, S. D., and J. E. Peters. 1973. Psychoeducational programming for children with minimal brain dysfunctions. *Ann. N. Y. Acad. Sci.* 205:46–51.

Connors, K. 2000. ADHD: Historical development and overview. *J. Att. Dis.* 3173–91.

Cox, D. J., R. L. Merkel, M. Moore, F. Thorndike, C. Muller, and B. Kovatchev. 2006. Benefits of stimulant therapy with OROS methylphenidate versus mixed amphetamine salts extended release in improving the driving performance of adolescent drivers with attention-deficit/hyperactivity disorder. *Pediatrics* 18:e704–10.

Eisenberg, L. (Moderator), and T. N. Gates (Moderator). 1973. General discussion. *Ann. N. Y. Acad. Sci.* 205:61–4.

Faraone, S. V., J. Biederman, and E. Mick. 2006. The age-dependent decline of attention deficit hyperactivity disorder: A meta-analysis of follow-up studies. *Psychol. Med.* 36:159–65.

Faraone, S. V., J. Biederman, T. Spencer, T. Wilens, L. J. Seidman, E. Mick, and A. E. Doyle. 2000. Attention-deficit/hyperactivity disorder in adults: An overview. *Biol. Psychiatry* 48:9–20.

Faraone, S. V., J. Sergeant, C. Gillberg, and J. Biederman. 2003. The worldwide prevalence of ADHD: Is it an American condition? *World Psychiatry* 2:104–14.

Faraone, S. V., R. H. Perlis, A. E. Doyle, J. W. Smoller, J. J. Goralnick, M. A. Holmgren, and P. Sklar. 2005. Molecular genetics of attention-deficit/hyperactivity disorder. *Biol. Psychiatry* 57:1313–23.

Gazzaniga, M. S. 1973. Brain theory and minimal brain dysfunction. *Ann. N. Y. Acad. Sci.* 205:89–92.

Hewett, F. M. 1973. Conceptual models for viewing minimal brain dysfunction: Developmental psychology and behavioral modification. *Ann. N. Y. Acad. Sci.* 205:38–45.

Katusic, S. K., W. J. Barbaresi, R. C. Colligan, A. L. Weaver, C. L. Leibson, and S. J. Jacobsen. 2005. Psychostimulant treatment and risk for substance abuse among young adults with a history of attention-deficit/hyperactivity disorder: A population-based, birth cohort study. *J. Child. Adolesc. Psychopharmacol* 15:764–76.

Kessler, R. C., L. Adler, R. Barkley R, J. Biederman, C. K. Conners, O. Demler, S. V. Faraone, L. L. Greenhill, M. J. Howes, K. Secnik, T. Spencer, T. B. Ustun, E. E. Walters, and A. M. Zaslavsky. 2006. The prevalence and correlates of adult ADHD in the United States: Results from the National Comorbidity Survey Replication. *Am. J. Psychiatry* 163:716–23.

Knights, R. M. 1973. Problems of criteria in diagnosis: A profile similarity approach. *Ann. N. Y. Acad. Sci.* 205:124–31.

McCabe, S. E., J. R. Knight, C. J. Teter, and H. Wechsler. 2005. Non-medical use of prescription stimulants among US college students: Prevalence and correlates from a national survey. *Addiction* 100:96–106.

Morrison, J. R., and M. A. Stewart. 1973. The psychiatric status of the legal families of adopted hyperactive children. *Arch. Gen. Psychiatry* 28:888–91.

The MTA Cooperative Group. 1999a. A 14-month randomized clinical trial of treatment strategies for attention-deficit/hyperactivity disorder. The MTA Cooperative Group. Multimodal Treatment Study of Children with ADHD.Arch Gen Psychiatry 56:1073–86.

The MTA Cooperative Group. 1999b. Moderators and mediators of treatment response for children with attention-deficit/hyperactivity disorder: the Multimodal Treatment Study of children with Attention-deficit/hyperactivity disorder. *Arch. Gen. Psychiatry* 56:1088–96.

Pearl, P. L., R. E. Weiss, and M. A. Stein. 2001. Medical mimics: Medical and neurological conditions simulating ADHD. *Ann. N. Y. Acad. Sci.* 931:97–112.

Prince, J. Making the most appropriate diagnosis of ADHD: Recognizing important behavioral elements. http://www.medscape.com/viewarticle/545471_9.

Reitan, R. M., and T. J. Boll. 1973. Neuropsychological correlates of minimal brain dysfunction. *Ann. N. Y. Acad. Sci.* 205:65–88.

Seidman, L. J., E. M. Valera, and N. Makris. 2005. Structural brain imaging of attention-deficit/hyperactivity disorder. *Biol. Psychiatry* 57:1263–72.

Seidman, L. J., E. M. Valera, N. Makris, M. C. Monuteaux, D. L. Boriel, K. Kelkar, D. N. Kennedy, V. S. Caviness, G. Bush, M. Aleardi, S. V. Faraone, and J. Biederman. 2006. Dorsolateral prefrontal and anterior cingulate cortex volumetric abnormalities in adults with attention-deficit/hyperactivity disorder identified by magnetic resonance imaging. *Biol. Psychiatry* 60:1071–80.

Sergeant, J. A., H. Geurts, S. Huijbregts, A. Scheres, and J. Oosterlaan. 2003. The top and the bottom of ADHD: A neuropsychological perspective. *Neurosci. Biobehav. Rev.* 27:583–92.

Sonuga-Burke, E. J. S. 2003. The dual pathway model of AD/HD: An elaboration of neuro-developmental characteristics. *Neurosci. Biobehav. Rev.* 27:593–604.

Strother, C. R. 1973. Minimal cerebral dysfunction: A historical overview. *Ann. N. Y. Acad. Sci.* 205:6–17.

Sussman, S., M. A. Pentz, D. Spruijt-Metz, and T. Miller. 2006. Misuse of "study drugs": Prevalence, consequences, and implications for policy. *Subst. Abuse. Treat. Prev. Policy* 1:1–15.

Swanson, J. M., M. Kinsbourne, J. Nigg, B. Lanphear, G. A. Stefanatos, N. Volkow, E. Taylor, B. J. Casey, F. X. Castellanos, and P. D. Wadhwa. 2007. Etiologic subtypes of attention-deficit/hyperactivity disorder: Brain imaging, molecular genetic and environmental factors and the dopamine hypothesis. *Neuropsychol. Rev.* 17:39–59.

Teter, C. J., S. E. McCabe, K. LaGrange, J. A. Cranford, and C. J. Boyd. 2006. Illicit use of specific prescription stimulants among college students: Prevalence, motives, and routes of administration. *Pharmacotherapy* 261:501–10.

Upadhyaya, H. P., K. Rose, W. Wang, K. O'Rourke, B. Sullivan, D. Deas, and K. T. Brady. 2005. Attention-deficit/hyperactivity disorder, medication treatment, and substance use patterns among adolescents and young adults. *J. Child. Adolesc. Psychopharmacol* 15:799–809.

van den Hoofdakker, B. J., L. van der Veen-Mulders, S. Sytema, P. M. Emmelkamp, R. B. Minderaa, and M. H. Nauta. 2007. Effectiveness of behavioral parent training for children with ADHD in routine clinical practice: A randomized controlled study. *J. Am. Acad. Child. Adolesc. Psychiatry* 46:1263–71.

Volkow, N. D., G. J. Wang, J. S. Fowler, and Y. S. Ding. 2005. Imaging the effects of methylphenidate on brain dopamine: New model on its therapeutic actions for attention-deficit/hyperactivity disorder. *Biol. Psychiatry* 57:1410–5.

Volkow, N., G. J. Wang, J. Newcorn, J. S. Fowler, F. Telang, M. V. Solanto, J. Logan, C. Wong, Y. Ma, J. M. Swanson, K. Schulz, and K. Pradhan. 2007. Neuroimaging investigation of the brain dopamine transporter (DAT) in ADHD. *NeuroImage* 34:1182–90.

Volkow, N. D., G. J. Wang, J. S. Fowler, F. Telang, L. Maynard, and J. Logan. 2004. Evidence that methylphenidate enhances the saliency of a mathematical task by increasing dopamine in the human brain. *Am. J. Psychiatry* 161:1173–80.

Weiss, M. D., and J. R. Weiss. 2004. A guide to the treatment of adults with ADHD. *J. Clin. Psychiatry* 65(Suppl. 3):27–37.

Wender, P. H. 1973. Some speculations concerning a possible biochemical basis of minimal brain dysfunction. *Ann. N. Y. Acad. Sci.* 205:18–28.

Wender, P. H., L. E. Wolf, and J. Wasserstein. 2001. Adults with ADHD: An overview. *Ann. N. Y. Acad. Sci.* 931:1–16.

Wilens, T. E., A. L. Hahesy, J. Biederman, E. Bredin, S. Tanguay, A. Kwon, and S. V. Faraone. 2005. Influence of parental SUD and ADHD on ADHD in their offspring: Preliminary results from a pilot-controlled family study. *Am. J. Addict.* 14:179–87.

Wilens, T. E., J. Biederman, and E. Mick. 1998. Does ADHD affect the course of substance abuse? Findings from a sample of adults with and without ADHD. *Am. J. Addict.* 7:156–63.

Wilens, T. E., J. Biederman, E. Mick, S. V. Faraone, and T. Spencer. 1997. Attention deficit hyperactivity disorder (ADHD) is associated with early onset substance use disorders. *J. Nerv. Ment. Dis.* 185:475–82.

Wilens, T. E., J. Biederman, and T. J. Spencer. 2002. Attention deficit/hyperactivity disorder across the lifespan. *Ann. Rev. Med.* 53:113–31.

Wilens, T. E., M. Gignac, A. Swezey, M. C. Monuteaux, and J. Biederman. 2006. Characteristics of adolescents and young adults with ADHD who divert or misuse their prescribed medications. *J. Am. Acad. Child. Adolesc. Psychiatry* 45:408–14.

Wilens, T. E., S. V. Faraone, and J. Biederman. 2004. Attention-deficit/hyperactivity disorder in adults. *JAMA* 292:619–23.

Wilens, T. E., S. V. Faraone, J. Biederman, and S. Gunawardene. 2003. Does stimulant therapy of attention-deficit/hyperactivity disorder beget later substance abuse? A meta-analytic review of the literature. *Pediatrics* 111:179–85.

Work, H. 2001. George Lathrop Bradley and the war over Ritalin. *Cosmos Journal*, September 11.

Zametkin, A. J., and J. L. Rapoport. 1987. Neurobiology of attention deficit disorder with hyperactivity: Where have we come in 50 years? *J. Am. Acad. Child. Adolesc. Psychiatry* 26:676–86.

WEB RESOURCES

http://www.aacap.org
http://aappolicy.aappublications.org
http://www.chad.org
http://www.drugabuse.gov/pubs/teaching/largegifs/slide-5.gif
http://www.fda.gov/cder
http://www.nimh.nih.gov/science-news/2007/brain-matures-a-few-years-late-in-adhd-but-follows-normal-pattern.shtml

Index

Still, George Frederic, M.D.,
8, 9
Stimulant medication(s), 10, 11, 12,
34, 36, 39, 44, 50, 56–61, 65, 73,
75, 88, 101
Substance abuse/dependence, 25, 48,
72–75, 80, 94, 100

Teacher, 17, 19, 20, 21, 23, 24, 27, 29,
30, 43, 65, 68, 74
Teen pregnancy, 79, 80, 100
Tic/Tic disorder(s), 59

Toxins, 34
TV, 19, 20, 35, 85

U.S. Food and Drug Administration
(FDA) 40, 41, 43–45, 57, 58, 61, 88, 89
United States Centers for Disease
Control and Prevention (CDC), 14

Video game, 19, 79

World Health Organization Adult
ADHD Self-Report Scale (ASRS
v1.1), 92, 94, 95

About the Author

PAUL GRAVES HAMMERNESS is the Scientific Coordinator for Pediatric ADHD research at the Clinical and Research Program in Pediatric Psychopharmacology, Massachusetts General Hospital, Harvard Medical School. He is also consulting physician in Child and Adolescent Psychiatry at Newton Wellesley Hospital.